the really hungry
VEGETARIAN STUDENT COOKBOOK

the really hungry
VEGETARIAN STUDENT COOKBOOK

HOW TO EAT WELL ON A BUDGET

RYLAND PETERS & SMALL
LONDON • NEW YORK

Senior Designer Iona Hoyle
Commissioning Editor Stephanie Milner
Production Sarah Kulasek-Boyd
Art Director Leslie Harrington
Editorial Director Julia Charles

Indexer Hilary Bird

First published in 2014.This edition published
in 2018 by Ryland Peters & Small
20–21 Jockey's Fields
London WC1R 4BW
and
341 E 116th St
New York NY 10029

www.rylandpeters.com

Text © Ghillie Basan, Jordan Bourke, Chloe Coker &
Jane Montgomery, Ross Dobson, Felipe Fuentes Cruz
& Ben Fordham, Tonia George, Nicola Graimes, Amanda
Grant, Dunja Gulin, Hannah Miles, Louise Pickford,
Annie Rigg, Jennie Shapter, Laura Washburn and
Ryland Peters & Small 2014, 2018

Design and photographs © Ryland Peters
& Small 2014

ISBN: 978-1-78879-046-8

10 9 8 7 6 5 4 3 2 1

A CIP record for this book is available from
the British Library.

US Library of Congress Cataloging-in-Publication data
has been applied for.

Printed and bound in China

NOTES:

★ Both British (Metric) and American (Imperial plus
US cups) are included in these recipes, however it is
important to work with one set of measurements and
not alternate between the two within a recipe.

★ All spoon measurements are level, unless
otherwise specified.

★ Ovens should be preheated to the specified
temperature. Recipes in this book were tested
using a regular oven. If using a fan-assisted oven,
follow the manufacturer's instructions for
adjusting temperatures.

★ To sterilize preserving jars, wash them in hot, soapy
water and rinse in boiling water. Place in a large
saucepan or pot and cover with hot water. With the
saucepan lid on, bring the water to a boil and continue
boiling for 15 minutes. Turn off the heat and leave the
jars in the hot water until just before they are to be
filled. Invert the jars onto a clean dish towel to dry.
Sterilize the lids for 5 minutes, by boiling or according
to the manufacturer's instructions. Jars should be filled
and sealed while they are still hot.

★ All eggs are medium UK/large US, unless
otherwise specified. Recipes containing raw or
partially cooked egg should not be served to the
very young, very old, anyone with a compromised
immune system or pregnant women.

★ Where a recipe calls for salt and black pepper,
use sea salt and freshly ground black pepper
if at all possible. They give the best flavour.

★ Cheeses started with animal rennet are not suitable
for strict vegetarians so read food labelling carefully
and, if necessary, check that the cheese you buy is
made with a non-animal (microbial) starter. Traditional
Parmesan is not vegetarian so we recommend a
vegetarian hard cheese (such as Gran Moravia which
has the same texture so is ideal for grating) or Parma
(a vegan product). There are an increasing number
of manufacturers who are now producing vegetarian
versions of traditionally non-vegetarian cheeses.
Check online for suppliers and stockists in your location.

contents

INTRODUCTION

If you're living away from home for the first time, you're going to want to know how to cook up a storm in the kitchen and this book is here to show you how. Whether you want to know how to make a stack of pancakes on a lazy Sunday morning, a warming bean stew to fight off those homesick blues or some tasty snacks for your movie night, this book has all you need. It will banish any fears you might have if you're new to cooking, and if you're already getting A grades in culinary arts, you're sure to find some fresh inspiration here. All the recipes are exciting, delicious and 100% vegetarian! Some are super-quick, while others need a little bit more time but are definitely worth the wait. Either way, this collection of stress-free recipes won't leave you hungry and will be cheaper and healthier than living on take-out. Check out all the hot tips in Kitchen Know-how on the following pages before you get started – they will make life a whole lot easier and ensure that you can always whip up something tasty, even with just a handful of good ingredients.

KITCHEN KNOW-HOW

The recipes in this book need the minimum of kitchen equipment. Some recipes, like the desserts, will require extras, e.g. a handheld electric whisk (which can be bought very cheaply), or a baking pan for brownies, etc. but you can go a long way with the following essential items:

CHECK LIST

HANDY INGREDIENTS

KITCHEN KIT

- ★ 2 or 3 sharp knives, including a serrated knife
- ☑ wooden spoon
- ★ fish/egg slice
- ☑ potato masher
- ★ garlic crusher
- ☑ pepper mill
- ★ can opener
- ☑ vegetable peeler
- ★ cheese grater
- ☑ 2 chopping boards
- ★ large mixing bowl
- ☑ sieve/strainer
- ★ colander
- ☑ 1 large and 1 medium saucepan
- ★ frying pan/skillet with a lid
- ☑ baking sheet

- ★ roasting pan
- ☑ ovenproof dish (Pyrex or ceramic)
- ★ measuring jug/pitcher
- ☑ weighing scales
- ★ a selection of airtight containers
- ☑ kettle
- ★ toaster
- ☑ kitchen foil
- ★ clingfilm/plastic wrap
- ☑ greaseproof paper
- ★ kitchen paper/paper towels
- ☑ cleaning stuff, including washing up liquid, sponges and multi-surface cleaner
- ★ dish towels
- ☑ oven gloves

- ★ sea salt
- ★ black peppercorns
- ★ olive oil
- ★ vegetable or sunflower oil
- ★ balsamic vinegar
- ★ red or white wine vinegar
- ★ dark or light soy sauce
- ★ tomato ketchup
- ★ mustard
- ★ mayonnaise
- ★ long grain rice
- ★ risotto rice
- ★ dried pasta, including spaghetti
- ★ couscous

- ★ stock cubes or bouillon powder
- ★ canned chopped tomatoes
- ★ a selection of canned beans, such as cannellini, pinto and kidney
- ★ a selection of dried and jarred vegetables such as sun-dried tomatoes, olives and capers
- ★ plain/all-purpose flour
- ★ self-raising/rising flour
- ★ sugar
- ★ tomato purée/paste
- ★ a selection of dried herbs, such as basil, oregano, rosemary and thyme

- ★ a selection of dried spices, such as curry powder, ground cumin, paprika, chilli/chili powder or dried chilli/hot pepper flakes
- ★ marmite
- ★ honey
- ★ butter or margarine
- ★ milk
- ★ onions
- ★ garlic
- ★ eggs
- ★ butter
- ★ cheese
- ★ tofu

FOOD SAFETY

⚜ **Always keep your kitchen clean!** Keep it tidy and disinfect work surfaces after use with a mild detergent or an antibacterial cleaner. Keep pets off surfaces and, as far as possible, keep them out of the kitchen.

⚜ Store food safely to avoid cross-contamination. Keep food in clean, dry, airtight containers, always store raw and cooked foods separately and wash utensils (and your hands) between preparing raw and cooked foods.

⚜ Wash your hands with hot, soapy water before and after handling food.

⚜ Never put hot food into a fridge or freezer, as this will increase the internal temperature to an unsafe level and may cause other foods to spoil. Cool leftover food quickly to room temperature, ideally by transferring it to a cold dish, then refrigerate or freeze. Cool large dishes such as stews by putting the dish in a sink of cold water. Stir occasionally then refrigerate once cool. During cooling, cover the food loosely with clingfilm/plastic wrap to protect it.

⚜ Don't use perishable food beyond the 'use-by' date as it could be a health risk. If you have any doubts about the food, discard it.

⚜ Reheated food must be piping hot throughout before consumption. Never reheat any type of food more than once.

⚜ If you are going to freeze food, freeze food that is in prime condition, on the day of purchase, or as soon as a dish is made and cooled. Freeze it quickly and in small quantities, if possible. Label and date food and keep plenty of supplies in the freezer.

⚜ Always leave a gap in the container when freezing liquids, so that there is enough room for the liquid to expand as it freezes.

⚜ Use proper oven gloves to remove hot dishes from the oven – don't just use a kitchen towel because you risk burning yourself. Kitchen towels are also a breeding ground for germs so only use them for drying, and wash them often.

⚜ Hard cheeses such as Gran Moravia and Parma will keep for up to 3 weeks if stored correctly. Once opened, fresh, soft cheeses such as cream cheese should be consumed within 3 days.

⚜ Leftover canned foods should be transferred to an airtight container, kept in the fridge and eaten within 2 days. Once cans are opened, the contents should be treated as fresh food.

⚜ The natural oils in chillies/chiles may cause irritation to your skin and eyes. When preparing them, wear disposable gloves or pull a small plastic bag over each hand, secured with an elastic band around the wrist, to create a glove.

⚜ If your kitchen is prone to over-heating, it is best to store eggs in their box in the fridge. Keep them pointed-end downwards and away from strong-smelling foods, as they can absorb odours. Always use by the 'best-before' date.

⚜ Wash hands before and after handling eggs, and discard any cracked and/or dirty eggs.

⚜ Cooked rice is a potential source of food poisoning. Cool leftovers quickly, then store in an airtight container in the fridge and use within 24 hours. Always reheat cooked cold rice to piping hot.

INGREDIENTS TIPS

◻ When substituting dried herbs for fresh, use roughly half the quantity the recipe calls for, as dried herbs have a more concentrated flavour.

◻ Chop leftover fresh herbs, spoon them into an ice-cube tray, top each portion with a little water and freeze. Once solid, put the cubes in a freezer bag. Seal, label and return to the freezer. Add the frozen herb cubes to soups, casseroles and sauces.

◻ The colour of a fresh chilli/chile is no indication of how hot it will be. Generally speaking, the smaller and thinner the chilli/chile, the hotter it will be.

◻ To reduce the heat of a fresh chilli, cut it in half lengthways, then scrape out and discard the seeds and membranes (or core). See also 'food safety' above for advice on handling chillies/chiles.

◻ Most vegetables keep best in the fridge, but a cool, dark place is also good if you lack fridge space. Potatoes should always be stored in the dark to avoid sprouting, making them inedible.

◻ To skin tomatoes, score a cross in the base of each one using a sharp knife. Put them in a heatproof bowl, cover with boiling water, leave for about 30 seconds, then transfer them to a bowl of cold water. When cool enough to handle, drain and peel off the skins with a knife.

◻ To clean leeks, trim them, then slit them lengthways about a third of the way through. Open the leaves a little and wash away any dirt from between the layers under cold running water.

◻ Store flour in its original sealed packaging or in an airtight container in a cool, dry, airy place. Ideally, buy and store small quantities at a time, to help avoid infestation of psocids (very small, barely visible, grey-brown insects), which may appear even in the cleanest of homes. If you do find these small insects in your flour, dispose of it immediately and wash and dry the container thoroughly. Never mix new flour with old.

◻ If you run out of self-raising/self-rising flour, sift together 2 teaspoons of baking powder with every 225 g/scant 2 cups plain/all-purpose flour. This will not be quite as effective but it is a good substitute.

◻ Store oils, well sealed, in a cool, dark, dry place, away from direct sunlight. They can be kept in the fridge, but oils such as olive oil tend to solidify and go cloudy in the fridge. If this happens, bring the oil back to room temperature before use.

◻ Small pasta tubes and twists such as penne and fusilli are good for chunky vegetable sauces.

◻ Dried pasta has a long shelf life and should be stored in its unopened packet or in an airtight container in a cool, dry place. Leftover cooked pasta should be kept in a sealed container in the fridge and used within 2 days. Ordinary cooked pasta does not freeze well on its own, but it freezes successfully in dishes such as lasagne. Allow 85–115 g/3–4 oz. of dried pasta per person.

◻ Pasta must be cooked in a large volume of salted, boiling water. Keep the water at a rolling boil throughout cooking. Once you have added the pasta to the boiling water, give it a stir, then cover the pan to help the water return to the boil as quickly as possible. Remove the lid once the water has started boiling again (to prevent the water boiling over), and stir occasionally. Check the manufacturer's instructions for cooking times. When it is ready, cooked pasta should be al dente – tender but with a slight resistance.

◻ Rice may be rinsed before cooking to remove tiny pieces of grit or excess starch. Most packaged rice is checked and clean, however, so rinsing it is unnecessary and will wash away nutrients. Risotto rice is not washed before use – rinse it under cold water until the water runs clear.

◻ As an accompaniment, allow 55–85 g/¼–⅓ cup uncooked rice per person or for a main like risotto, up to 115 g/½ cup.

KITCHEN WISDOM

■ To remove odours from a container that you want to use again, fill the container with hot water, then stir in 1 tablespoon baking powder. Leave it to stand overnight, then wash, rinse well and dry before use.

■ If you transfer foods from packages to storage containers, tape the food label onto the container so you can easily identify its contents and you have a record of the manufacturer's cooking instructions, if necessary. Make a note of the 'best-before' or 'use-by' date on the container, too.

■ Choose stackable containers to maximize storage space. Remember that square or rectangular containers make better use of shelf space than round or oval containers.

■ For convenient single servings, freeze portions of home-made soup in large, thick paper cups or small individual containers. Remove them from the freezer as required, defrost and reheat the soup thoroughly before serving.

■ To make salad dressings or vinaigrettes, put all the ingredients in a clean screw-top jar, seal and shake well. Alternatively, put the ingredients straight into the salad bowl and whisk together well, before adding the salad.

■ Spirits with an alcohol content of 35% or over can be kept in the freezer – this is ideal for those which should be served ice-cold.

■ If you are short of space in the kitchen, cover the sink with a piece of wood cut to size or a large chopping board to create an extra work surface when the sink is not in use.

MICROWAVE SAFETY

■ The more food you are cooking, and the colder it is, the longer it will take to cook in a microwave.

■ Many foods need to be covered during microwaving. Use microwave-safe clingfilm/plastic wrap, a plate or a lid. Pierce clingfilm/plastic wrap, or leave a gap at one side if using a plate or lid, to allow excess steam to escape.

■ Never operate a microwave when it is empty, as the microwaves will bounce back to and damage the oven components.

■ Be careful when stirring heated liquids in a container in the microwave, as they can bubble up without warning.

■ After food has been removed from the microwave, it will continue to cook due to the residual heat within the food, so adhere to standing times when they are given in recipes.

■ Use a microwave with a built-in turntable if possible, and make sure that you turn or stir the food several times during cooking to ensure even cooking throughout. The food towards the outer edges usually cooks first.

■ Metal containers, china with a metallic trim, foil or crystal glass (which contains lead) should not be used in a microwave. Metal reflects microwaves and may damage the oven components. Microwave-safe plastic containers, ovenproof glass and ceramic dishes are all suitable, as is most household glazed china. Paper plates and kitchen paper can be used to reheat food for short periods.

VEGETARIAN KNOW-HOW

There are many definitions of a vegetarian diet and many reasons why people choose to follow the diet that they do: ethical, environmental, health, religious, financial or simply personal choice. Vegetarian diets can be either simply meat-free or some people may choose to also exclude either eggs or dairy (or both), or eat a totally vegan diet, free from all animal products, including honey. It is important that when food groups are removed from a person's diet, the balance of key dietary components are considered and maintained.

KEY NUTRIENTS IN THE VEGETARIAN DIET

★ **carbohydrate and fibre/fiber** are usually plentiful in a good vegetarian or vegan diet – eating a variety of fruit and vegetables, including skins where possible, along with bran, potatoes and wholegrains should provide everything needed.

★ **protein** is essential in any diet. Not only is it necessary to the body for growth and repair and the production of enzymes and hormones, it also makes you feel full. An average person should eat around 45–55 g/1½–2 oz. of protein a day. In a meat-free diet, it can be harder to find complete sources of protein. This can be combatted by ensuring that you eat a variety of foods during the day and by mixing different sources of protein in one dish, such as grains with pulses, nuts or seeds. Whilst soya/soy, eggs, milk and cheese are all excellent sources of protein, they can be over-used. Consider using a variety of lentils, beans, chickpeas and wholegrains in your cooking. Quinoa is a good source of protein added to salads or used as a substitute for rice. A sprinkling of chopped nuts or seeds is a great way to add extra protein to any dish.

★ **key vitamins and minerals** can sometimes be lacking in vegetarian diets. As well as what you are eating, think about the cooking process – try to eat a substantial amount of raw vegetables or use cooking methods such as steaming and blanching to retain as much goodness as possible. As well as eating a broad range of fruit and vegetables, for those who eat dairy and/or eggs, a lot of essential vitamins (A, B2, B12 and D) can be found in milk and eggs. For those who do not eat dairy, fortified foods such as breakfast cereals and soya/soy milk are good sources of vitamins, as are green vegetables. Vitamin C, found in citrus fruit, is usually plentiful in vegetarian and vegan diets. Not only is it important for the body, it also helps to release minerals from pulses and vegetables and helps the body to absorb iron – try squeezing some lemon juice over a salad or adding it to a dressing.

★ **calcium** can easily be found in dairy produce, but those following a dairy-free diet should ensure that they include plenty of green vegetables (such as kale and broccoli), sesame seeds, beans and nuts in their diet. Calcium can also be found in soya/soy milk and fruit juices.

★ **iron** can be lacking in meat-free diets, but eating a combination of leafy green vegetables, dried fruits, beans, nuts, seeds and tofu will combat this.

★ **fatty acids** generally vegetarian diets are fairly low in saturated fat. Dairy products are a good source of fatty acids, although it is important not to be over-reliant on them. Seeds, walnuts and soya/soy are good sources of fat. Why not also try using different oils – nut oils, rapeseed and linseed oils can all be used both for cooking and flavouring.

BOOSTING BREAKFASTS

Mushrooms in a creamy parsley sauce are simply irresistible and make just as good a main meal as a hearty breakfast. A few thickly sliced tomatoes, quickly seared in some oil in a pan and a poached or fried egg are the perfect accompaniments.

MUSHROOMS
on toast

Heat the butter and oil in a non-stick frying pan/skillet set over a low heat. Add the mushrooms and cook for about 10 minutes, stirring occasionally, until tender and golden.

Meanwhile, crack the eggs into a separate non-stick frying pan/skillet set over a high heat and fry for 3–4 minutes until crisp underneath. Add the tomatoes to the pan cut side down and fry for a minute to char the edges. Remove from the heat and keep warm until you are ready to serve.

Turn up the heat and stir in the garlic (if using) and parsley and cook for about a minute. Add the cream and simmer gently for 2–3 minutes. Season to taste.

Serve immediately the mushrooms in their sauce on the toast with an egg and some charred tomatoes.

SERVES 2

1 tablespoon unsalted butter

2–3 tablespoons vegetable oil

500 g/1 lb. mushrooms, washed and quartered

1 garlic clove, crushed (optional)

1 teaspoon dried parsley

150 ml/⅔ cup single/light cream

salt and black pepper

To serve

2 slices wholemeal/whole-wheat bread, toasted

2 eggs

4 tomatoes, halved

These homemade baked beans are utterly delicious.
They are sweet and smoky and way better than
canned beans! Pile them on top of toasted and
buttered wholemeal/whole-wheat bread, or serve
with hash browns if you feel really naughty.

homemade
BAKED BEANS

If using dried beans, put them in large bowl. Add enough water to cover by 8 cm/3 inches and let stand overnight. The next day, drain the beans and put them in a saucepan or pot filled with water set over a medium–high heat. Bring to the boil and simmer for 40 minutes until the beans are tender. Drain.

Preheat the oven to 150°C (300°F) Gas 2.

Put the butter in a large ovenproof dish set over a medium heat and fry the bacon until it has browned. Add the onions, paprika and mustard. Reduce the heat to low, cover with a lid and cook for 5 minutes longer, stirring occasionally.

Add the prepared or canned beans, tomato purée, stock and season with salt and pepper. Cover with a lid and bake in the preheated oven for 2 hours.

Remove the dish from the oven and give everything a good stir. Add the maple syrup and taste to check the seasoning. Bake for a further 20 minutes with the lid off until the sauce has thickened.

Serve with hot buttered toast. Delish!

400 g/14 oz. dried beans or
2 x 400-g cans haricot/soldier,
white navy or pinto beans

2 tablespoons butter

250 g/8 oz. vegetarian bacon,
chopped

2 onions, chopped

1 teaspoon smoked paprika

2 teaspoons mustard

1 tablespoon tomato purée/paste

250 ml/1 cup hot vegetable stock

salt and black pepper

6 tablespoons maple syrup

8 slices wholemeal/whole-wheat
bread, toasted and buttered

SERVES 4

Lectures all morning? Long wait till lunch? Try this rich and sticky French toast to kick-start your day. Sliced bread tends to be thin but if using bread from a whole loaf, you may need to add a bit more milk to ensure there is enough.

cinnamon
FRENCH TOAST

SERVES 2

2 eggs

4 tablespoons milk

a pinch of sugar

½–1 teaspoon ground cinnamon

unsalted butter and vegetable oil, for cooking

4 slices organic wholemeal/whole-wheat bread

Caramelized apples

2–3 tablespoons sultanas/golden raisins

3 tablespoons butter

1 teaspoon vegetable oil

2 small red apples, cut into cubes

1 large apple, coarsely chopped

1 generous tablespoon dark soft brown sugar

To serve(optional)

2–3 tablespoons finely chopped nuts, such as hazelnuts, almonds or pecans

maple syrup or honey

plain yogurt

First prepare the apples. If the sultanas/golden raisins are not plump, soak them in a small bowl of boiling water for a few minutes. Drain and set aside.

Put the butter and oil in a small non-stick frying pan/skillet set over a medium–high heat until just sizzling. Add the apple pieces and sugar, stir to coat and cook for 8–10 minutes, stirring occasionally, until just tender and lightly browned all over. Add the sultanas/golden raisins after 5 minutes cooking time. Set aside.

To make the French toast, whisk together the eggs, milk, sugar and cinnamon in a shallow dish, until well blended.

Heat the butter and oil together in a non-stick frying pan/skillet large enough to hold at least 2 slices of bread side by side set over a medium heat.

While the butter is heating, dip a slice of bread in the egg mixture, pricking it lightly with a fork to help absorption. Turn carefully and soak the other side. Transfer quickly to the pan. Repeat for the other slice and cook for 2–3 minutes on each side. Once cooked, keep the toasts warm while you cook the remaining slices in the same way, adding a little more butter and oil to the pan.

To serve, cut the toasts in half. Divide the apple mixture between the plates, mounding it on top of the bread. Sprinkle with the nuts and serve, with maple syrup or honey and a dollop of plain yogurt.

Get off to a healthy start in the morning with these easy and nutritious pancakes. They are the perfect post-party breakfast, packed full of goodness with salty melted butter and a drizzle of sweet maple syrup.

multigrain
PANCAKES

Put all of the dry ingredients in a mixing bowl and set aside.

Whisk together the milk, eggs and oil in a separate bowl or jug/pitcher. Then pour the milk mixture onto the flour mixture and beat until blended but still a little lumpy.

Heat a large non-stick frying pan/skillet over a medium–high heat and wipe or brush lightly with a little vegetable oil. Pour ladlefuls of the pancake batter into the hot pan and cook until bubbles begin to appear on the surface. Turn the pancakes over and cook for 1–2 minutes on the other side.

Once cooked, keep the pancakes warm while you cook the remaining batter in the same way, adding a little more oil to the pan as necessary. Repeat until all of the batter has been used.

Serve immediately with butter and maple syrup.

120 g/¾ cup wholemeal/whole-wheat flour

65 g/½ cup oat bran

85 g/1½ cups plain/all-purpose flour

45 g/¼ cup cornmeal

1 teaspoon baking powder

½ teaspoon bicarbonate of soda/baking soda

a pinch of salt

400 ml/1¾ cups milk

2 eggs

2 tablespoons vegetable oil

MAKES ABOUT 15 PANCAKES

Porridge is the ultimate brain food. Whip this up before an exam or when you need to pull an all-day or all-night session in the library. Spiced apple and blackberries add essential vitamins to give you that extra zing!

apple & blackberry
PORRIDGE

100 g/¾ cup quick-cook rolled oats

250 ml/1 cup whole milk, plus a little extra to thin

a pinch of salt

75 g/½ cup (golden) raisins

1 tablespoon butter

2 apples, cored and sliced

3 tablespoons demerara/turbinado sugar

a pinch of ground cinnamon

100 g/1 cup blackberries

SERVES 4

Put the oats in a saucepan or pot set over a medium heat and add the milk and 250 ml/1 cup water. Add a pinch of salt, cover with a lid and slowly bring the mixture to the boil. Once the mixture is bubbling, reduce the heat, add the raisins and cook for 2–3 minutes, stirring occasionally. The porridge should be thick and creamy. Remove from the heat and let stand with a lid on while you cook the apples.

Put the butter in a frying pan/skillet set over high heat until it bubbles. Stir in the apples, sugar and cinnamon and cook for 2–3 minutes until the underside begins to caramelize. Then flip the slices over so the other side gets a chance to become golden too. Finally, add the blackberries and heat for a couple of minutes just so they warm through a little.

Meanwhile, spoon the porridge into bowls and stir in a little cold milk to stop it becoming too thick. Spoon the caramelized apples and blackberries on top and serve while still piping hot.

Making your own granola is both cheap and easy to do. You can make a large batch and store it in an airtight container using any dried fruit and nuts that you have to hand.

crunchy oat
GRANOLA

MAKES 8 SERVINGS

Preheat the oven to 150°C (300°F) Gas 2.

Put the oats, nuts, seeds, coconut, salt and mixed/apple pie spice in a large mixing bowl, add the grated apple and stir until well combined. Set aside.

Put the sugar, oil and honey in a saucepan or pot set over low heat and stir until melted. Remove from the heat and pour over the dry ingredients. Stir the mixture until well combined.

Spread the granola evenly on the largest baking sheet you have, taking care not to heap the mixture to ensure that it cooks evenly. Bake in the preheated oven for 40–45 minutes, stirring every 10 minutes, until the granola is golden.

Add the dried fruit and bake for a further 5 minutes. Take care not to let it burn. Remove the granola from the oven and let cool.

Serve your homemade granola with a large spoonful each of plain yogurt and fruit jam/jelly or store it in a sterilized glass jar with an airtight lid until ready to eat.

500 g/5 cups rolled oats

150 g/1⅓ cups mixed chopped nuts

150 g/1¼ cups mixed seeds

50 g dessicated/shredded coconut (optional)

½ teaspoon salt (optional)

2 teaspoons mixed/apple pie spice

2 eating apples, grated with skin on

2 tablespoons dark brown sugar

4 tablespoons vegetable, sunflower, canola or hazelnut oil

8 tablespoons runny honey, maple syrup or golden/light corn syrup

150 g/1 cup choppped mixed dried fruit of your choice

To Serve

plain yogurt

fruit jam/jelly

a sterilized glass jar with an airtight lid (see page 4)

The nuts in these bars boost their nutritional value, as do the seeds. Perfect for baking in the evening to take with you when you're running late for a lecture or need a mid-morning boost before lunch. You can use any jam/jelly you like.

fruit & nut
BARS

160 g/1 cup wholemeal/whole-wheat flour

230 g/1½ cups plain/all-purpose flour

230 g/1 cup caster/granulated sugar

175 g/1½ sticks unsalted butter

a pinch of salt

6–8 tablespoons fruit jam/jelly

110 g/1 cup mixed unsalted nuts, such as walnuts, pecans and hazelnuts

2–3 tablespoons sunflower seeds

a 20 x 30-cm/8 x 12-inch baking sheet, greased and lined with baking parchment

Preheat the oven to 180°C (350°F) Gas 4.

Put both the flours, sugar, butter and salt into a food processor and pulse to coarse crumbs. Alternatively, mix in a large bowl, using your fingertips to work the butter into the flour mixture.

Spread just over half of the mixture evenly over the prepared baking sheet, patting it down firmly. Then spread the fruit jam/jelly on top in an even layer.

Add the nuts and seeds to the remaining flour mixture and stir to combine. Sprinkle loosely over the fruit layer to cover entirely.

Bake in the preheated oven for 25–35 minutes, until just brown around the edges. Let cool slightly on the baking sheet then slice into bars.

Store in an airtight container for 7–10 days or wrap each bar individually in foil to have on the go.

MAKES 12–15 BARS

This is one for the scientists. Making crumpets is like conducting an experiment — you may not understand the chemical reaction happening, but it's great to see the crumpets bubble, ready to receive melted butter in their pockets.

CRUMPETS

Pour the milk and sugar into a saucepan or pot set over a medium heat to warm through. Remove from the heat, scatter over the yeast and set aside for 10 minutes until foamy on the surface.

Meanwhile, sift the flours and salt into a mixing bowl and add the oil and then the wet, foamy mixture. Beat with an electric handheld whisk for 3 minutes, or until smooth. Cover with clingfilm/plastic wrap and leave for 1½–2 hours, until the batter has doubled in size and is covered in tiny bubbles.

Mix the water and bicarbonate of/baking soda in a separate bowl until dissolved. Beat this into the risen batter until smooth. Cover again and let rise for a further 20 minutes.

Put the metal rings on a lightly oiled hot non-stick frying pan/skillet set over a low heat. Spoon 2 tablespoons of batter into each ring so they are half full. Cook for 5–7 minutes until the surface is pockmarked and dry around the edges. Slide the rings off, flip the crumpets over and cook until pale gold. Once cooked, keep the crumpets warm while you cook the remaining batter in the same way, adding a little more oil to the pan. Repeat until all of the batter has been used.

Serve buttered with fruit jam/jelly if desired.

500 ml/2 cups whole milk

1 teaspoon sugar

1 tablespoon fast-action dried yeast

200 g/1½ cups strong white/bread flour

200 g/1½ cups plain/all-purpose flour

1 teaspoon salt

2 tablespoons sunflower oil, plus extra for the pan

250 ml/1 cup warm water

½ teaspoon bicarbonate of/baking soda

an electric handheld whisk

4 x 8-cm/3-inch metal rings, greased

MAKES 12

Juicy melon and cool cucumber are blended to make a super-cooling and satisfying summer drink. Stem ginger adds a nice spicy kick and works well with pear juice for an alternative to the melon here – the two flavours just seem to have a natural affinity.

melon, cucumber, & ginger
FRAPPÉ

½ galia melon, about 1 kg/3 lbs., deseeded

½ cucumber, peeled and chopped

1 tablespoon chopped stem ginger, plus 1 tablespoon syrup from the jar

freshly squeezed juice of ½ lime

170 g/1 cup ice

Scoop out the flesh of the melon and put into a blender or food processor. Add the cucumber, stem ginger with its syrup, lime juice and ice. Whizz until the ice has broken down and the frappé is smooth.

Divide the mixture between 2 glasses or tumblers to serve, or cover and keep in the fridge for up to 2 days.

Variation
Pear, cucumber and ginger are a refreshing alternative to the melon in this recipe. Try it out when fresh pears are in season.

SERVES 2

There's nothing like a good Bloody Mary after a big night out: it seems to get the blood pumping and cure any feelings of drowsiness. A Virgin Mary is a great healthy alternative to start the day without the booze factor.

BLOODY MARY

Mix all the ingredients together in a jug/pitcher. Taste and adjust the seasonings if necessary, adding more heat, pepper or lime as you wish.

Add a couple of handfuls of ice to the jug/pitcher and serve with a stack of tumblers. Add a celery stick to taller glasses to stir with.

Variation
To make a Virgin Mary leave out the vodka but squeeze in some more lime so you get more of a tang.

150 ml/⅔ cup vodka

450 ml/1 cup pure tomato juice

½ teaspoon horseradish sauce

1 teaspoon Worcestershire sauce

4 dashes Tabasco sauce

¼ teaspoon celery salt

½ teaspoon cracked black pepper

2 limes, cut into small wedges

ice, to serve

4 celery sticks (optional)

SERVES 4

LUNCHBOX HEROES

Wraps make a welcome change from ordinary
sandwiches are are easily wrapped to have on
the move. Flour tortillas make the best wrapper
but large supermarkets often stock other types
of flatbreads made especially for wraps.

avocado & chickpea
WRAP

Working one at a time, put a tortilla on the work surface.
Sprinkle a quarter of the chickpeas on top, in a line down the
middle. Mash lightly with a fork, spreading out in a half-moon
shape towards one edge of the tortilla.

Cover this with a generous spoonful of cottage cheese and
arrange a few slices of avocado in a line down the middle.

Sprinkle over a small handful of diced tomato, a little grated
cheddar and some lettuce. Then squeeze over a little lemon
juice, season lightly with salt and pepper and finish with a
drizzle of oil.

To roll up the wrap, starting from the edge with the filling,
begin rolling to enclose the filling. Cut in half and serve
immediately, with the seam-side down.

4 wholemeal/whole-wheat
tortillas or other wraps

410-g/14-oz. can chickpeas
drained and rinsed

4 generous spoonfuls cottage
cheese

1 ripe avocado, peeled, pitted/
stoned and thinly sliced (see
method on page 38)

1 tomato, deseeded and diced

3–4 tablespoons grated
vegetarian cheddar

a few handfuls of shredded Little
Gem/Bibb lettuce

freshly squeezed juice of ½ lemon

olive oil, for drizzling

salt and black pepper

MAKES 2–4
SERVINGS

Sandwiches are easy to pack and take on the move. Small plastic or stainless steel, lidded containers can be reused and keep your lunch fresh.

super-nutritious SANDWICHES

Ricotta & Pesto Bagel
Spread the pesto on the bottom half of the seeded bagel before spooning ricotta cheese on top. Season with salt and pepper. Lay fresh spinach leaves across the bagel before topping with the other half of the bagel.

Carrot & Hoummus Rolls
Spread a thin layer of hoummus on the bottom halves of each roll and top with the grated carrot. Add a sprinkling of pine nuts/kernels or sesame seeds for a 'super grain' boost and top with the lids of each roll.

Cream Cheese Sandwich
Spread cream cheese on one slice of bread and top with chopped cucumber and tomato. Add the watercress strands and top with the second slice of bread.

Note
Serve each sandwich immediately or wrap in paper towels before putting into an airtight container. Store in the fridge if possible or consume within 3 hours.

Ricotta & Pesto Bagel
1 seeded bagel, sliced in half

2 teaspoons Pesto (see page 54)

1 tablespoon ricotta

a handful of fresh spinach leaves

salt and black pepper

Carrot & Hoummus Rolls
2 wholemeal/whole-wheat rolls, sliced in half

2 tablespoons hoummus

finely grated carrots

pine nuts/kernels or sesame seeds (optional)

Cream Cheese Sandwich
2 slices seeded wholemeal/whole-wheat bread

1 tablespoon cream cheese

⅛ cucumber, deseeded and finely chopped

1 tomato, deseeded and finely chopped

a handful of watercress strands

The avocado is a great source of essential nutrients and protein, making it a go-to food for those on a vegetarian diet. They are super-healthy and make this sandwich super-smooth and delicious.

AVOCADO
& red pepper sandwich

2 avocados

freshly squeezed juice of ½ lemon

8 slices thick wholemeal/whole-wheat bread

butter, softened to spread (optional)

1 red (bell) pepper, seeds removed and finely chopped

salt and black pepper

Begin by preparing the avocados. Cut each fruit in half using a sharp knife, starting at the top and cutting round the stone/pit. Separate the two halves of each and set the stoned/pitted halves aside. Carefully cut into the stones/pits and twist to remove and discard. Finally peel the skin and cut the flesh into slices.

Mash the avocado with the lemon juice, and spread a quarter of the mixture onto your chosen bread.

Sprinkle the pepper over the top of the avocado and season with salt and pepper. Top each sandwich with a second slice of bread.

Serve the sandwiches immediately or wrap in paper towels before putting into an airtight container. Store in the fridge if possible or consume within 3 hours.

Variation
Roasted red (bell) pepper from a jar gives a richer flavour here, if preferred. Try adding capers and chopped olives for a more salty taste.

SERVES 4

Nothing beats an egg and cress sandwich. Soft, buttered bread with the protein boost of egg and peppery fresh cress is heaven on a plate!

EGG SANDWICHES

Egg mayonnaise with watercress or lettuce

Mash the boiled egg in a bowl and add the mayonnaise or salad cream. Season with black pepper and mix well. Spoon the mixture onto a slice of buttered bread and top with a handful of fresh watercress or lettuce, then a second slice of bread.

Egg mayonnaise with red pepper & cucumber

Mash the boiled egg in a bowl and add the chopped red (bell) pepper and a little finely chopped cucumber. Season with black pepper and mix well. Spoon the mixture onto a slice of buttered bread and top with a second slice of bread.

Note

Serve each sandwich immediately or wrap in paper towels before putting into an airtight container. Store in the fridge if possible or consume within 3 hours.

Egg mayonnaise with watercress or lettuce

1 egg, boiled, peeled and cooled

2 teaspoons mayonnaise or salad cream

a pinch of black pepper

2 slices thick wholemeal/whole-wheat bread

a handful of fresh watercress or lettuce

Egg mayonnaise with red pepper & cucumber

1 egg, boiled and mashed

¼ red (bell) pepper, deseeded and finely chopped

⅛ cucumber, desseeded and finely chopped

2 slices thick wholemeal/whole-wheat bread

EACH SERVES 1

This little nutritious salad with pinto beans and
crunchy taco pieces brings Mexico to the table.
It is a dry salad to keep the taco pieces crisp
but if you want a dressing, simply add a little
olive oil and freshly squeezed lime juice.

MEXICAN TACO SALAD

150 g/¾ cup dried pinto beans,
or 1 x 410-g/14-oz. can kidney
beans, drained and well rinsed

2 firm, ripe avocados, peeled,
pitted/stoned and sliced (see
method on page 38)

3 ripe tomatoes, deseeded and
thinly sliced

50 g/⅓ cup pitted black olives,
sliced

1 red onion, thinly sliced

1 crisp lettuce, such as iceberg,
shredded

a small bunch of fresh coriander/
cilantro, roughly chopped

8 stoneground yellow corn taco
shells

To serve

olive oil

1 lime, cut into wedges

Put the pinto beans in a bowl, cover with cold water and
let soak overnight. You could you canned kidney beans if
you are short of time and skip the next step.

The next morning, drain the beans and cook in a large
saucepan or pot of boiling water set over a medium–high
heat for 3–3½ hours, until tender, topping up the water
from time to time. Drain well and transfer to a large bowl.

Preheat the oven to 180°C (350°F) Gas 4.

Put the avocado and tomato slices in the bowl with the
beans. Add the olives, onion, lettuce and coriander/
cilantro and gently toss to combine.

Put the taco shells on a baking sheet and cook in the
preheated oven for 8–10 minutes, until crisp. When cool
enough to handle, roughly break each taco shell into
pieces and add to the bowl of salad. Toss to combine,
taking care not to break up the taco pieces.

Serve immediately with a drizzle of olive oil and a squeeze
of fresh lime if desired.

SERVES 4

This is a slight twist on a classic Greek salad. Butter beans are a staple of Greek cuisine but are usually served baked in a rich tomato sauce and served as part of a meze. Their delicate flavour works well here with tangy feta and olives.

GREEK SALAD
with butter beans

Put the tomatoes, olives, mint, parsley and beans in a large bowl and toss to combine.

Put the oil in a frying pan/skillet set over medium heat. Add the onions and garlic. When they start to sizzle in the oil, remove from the heat and pour over the tomato mixture. Stir in the lemon juice and add the feta. Season to taste with salt and pepper and toss well to combine. Set aside for 30 minutes to allow the flavours to infuse.

Toss again and serve at room temperature with the toasted bread and an extra drizzle of olive oil.

400 g/14 oz. cherry tomatoes, halved

50 g/½ cup kalamata olives, halved and pitted

a small bunch of fresh mint, roughly chopped

a small bunch of fresh flat-leaf parsley, finely chopped

2 x 410-g/14-oz. cans butter beans, drained and well rinsed

3 tablespoons olive oil, plus extra to serve

2 red onions, thinly sliced

2 garlic cloves, finely chopped

3 tablespoons freshly squeezed lemon juice

200 g/7 oz. feta cheese, cut into cubes

salt and black pepper

bread, sliced and lightly toasted, to serve

SERVES 4

Many recipes using pulses/legumes are Middle Eastern in origin, such as falafel, a popular street food. It is a pattie made using dried chickpeas or broad/fava beans or a combination of the two.

homemade
FALAFEL

150 g/¾ cup dried broad/fava beans, preferably peeled

220 g/1 cup dried chickpeas

1 large onion, chopped

8 garlic cloves, chopped

a small bunch of fresh flat-leaf parsley, chopped

a bunch of fresh coriander/cilantro, chopped

1 tablespoon ground cumin

2 teaspoons ground coriander

¼ teaspoon chilli powder

2 teaspoons salt

vegetable oil, for shallow frying

To serve

flat breads

250 ml/1 cup store-bought tzatziki or minted yogurt

MAKES ABOUT 30

Put the broad/fava beans in a bowl, cover with cold water and let soak overnight. Put the chickpeas in a separate bowl and repeat. You could use canned broad/fava beans and chickpeas if you are short of time.

Put the broad/fava beans in a food processor and blend to a fine crumb. Transfer to a large bowl and repeat with the chickpeas, adding them to the bowl too.

Now add the onion, garlic, parsley and fresh coriander/cilantro to the food processor and blend until well combined. Add this mixture to the beans and chickpeas with the cumin, ground coriander, chilli powder and salt. Stir well then set aside for 30 minutes.

Heat enough oil in a frying pan/skillet to come about 2½ cm/1 inch up the side over a low–medium heat. The oil is ready to cook in when the surface is shimmering and a pinch of the mixture sizzles on contact with the oil.

Using two tablespoons, form the mixture into oval patties. Drop directly into the hot oil and cook for 2–3 minutes, turning halfway through until golden and crispy. Once cooked, keep the falafel warm while you cook the remaining mixture in the same way.

Serve the falafel wrapped in flat breads and dressed with tzatziki or minted yogurt.

BUON APPETITO

Bruschettas are a classic Italian antipasti. With a choice of toppings you can whip up a platter of delicious, fresh-tasting bites in no time.

mini BRUSCHETTAS

Follow the method on page 55 to make your own pesto or simply load up your toasts with store-bought pesto, drizzle with olive oil and sprinkle with salt and pepper.

To make the olive and caper topping, whizz the olives, garlic, capers, lemon zest, chilli/hot red pepper flakes, parsley, sugar and olive oil in a food processor. Season to taste with lemon juice, salt, pepper and an extra pinch of sugar if the olives have a particularly sour edge. Don't add salt before tasting, as olives are usually salty enough already.

For the roasted tomato and pepper topping, preheat the oven to 200°C (400°F) Gas 6. Halve the peppers and put them with the tomatoes, and garlic on the prepared baking sheet, sprinkle with salt and drizzle with olive oil, and cook in the preheated oven for 10–15 minutes. Remove the garlic when and set aside. Continue to cook the tomatoes and peppers for another 10 minutes, then remove the tomatoes and set aside. Cook the peppers for a final 5 minutes until their skins have coloured, remove from the oven and put them in a sealed plastic bag so their skins are easily removed. Once the tomatoes are cool, remove and discard the skins and put the flesh in a bowl. Squeeze the garlic cloves out of their skins into the same bowl. Once the peppers are cool, remove from the plastic bag and peel away their skins. Roughly chop the peppers and tomatoes and put them back in the bowl. Mix to combine and season to taste with salt and pepper.

Serve the assorted toppings on lightly toasted or grilled ciabatta slices, finish with a small drizzle of olive oil. Assemble just before you are ready to serve, otherwise the bread will become soggy.

1 ciabatta or baguette, sliced and lightly toasted or grilled

olive oil, for drizzling

Classic pesto topping

Pesto (page 55)

salt and pepper

Olive & caper topping

500g/4 cups pitted black olives, finely chopped

2 garlic cloves, crushed

4 tablespoons capers, well rinsed

grated zest and juice of 2 lemons

1 teaspoon chilli/hot red pepper flakes

4 tablespoons/¼ cup dried parsley

a pinch of sugar

a splash of olive oil

Roasted tomato & pepper topping

2 red (bell) peppers, deseeded

400 g/14 oz. fresh plum tomatoes

2 garlic cloves, unpeeled

6 tablespoons olive oil

a baking sheet lined with foil

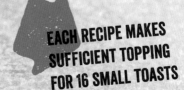

EACH RECIPE MAKES SUFFICIENT TOPPING FOR 16 SMALL TOASTS

This soft focaccia-style bread is a great accompaniment to soup or salad. You can experiment with your own choice of flavoursome toppings too.

Italian-style
TEAR & SHARE BREAD

Put the flour and salt in a large bowl and mix together. Stir the dried yeast and sugar through the flour and set aside. Make a well in the centre and add the olive oil. Then add 185 ml/¾ cup of the lukewarm water. Quickly stir together to form a soft dough. If the dough seems dry, add the remaining water.

Tip the dough onto a lightly floured surface and knead for 10 minutes until the dough becomes smooth and elastic. To test if the dough is well kneaded, make a ball and press with your finger. If the indent springs back, the dough has been sufficiently kneaded and is ready rise.

Put the dough back in the bowl and cover with lightly oiled clingfilm/plastic wrap. Leave to rise in a warm place for about 45 minutes until doubled in size. Make another indent in the dough to test if it is ready. The indent should remain.

Knock back/punch down your dough by kneading for 1–2 minutes. Stretch it out into a large rectangle on the floured baking sheet to about 2 cm/¾ inch thick. Cover again with lightly oiled clingfilm/plastic wrap and set aside to rise/prove for about 30–40 minutes. It should double in size.

Preheat the oven to 200°C (400°F) Gas 6.

Uncover and press your finger into the dough to make regular indents until the whole loaf is a mass of dimples, then sprinkle the bread with olive oil and salt flakes. Add the cherry tomatoes, pesto and rosemary. Bake in the top of the oven for 25–30 minutes, adding the onion after 10 minutes. It should be golden brown, feel quite light when you pick it up, and have a hollow sound to it when you tap the bottom.

450 g/1 lb. white strong/bread flour (between 3⅓–3½ cups)

2 teaspoons salt

7–g/¼-oz. fast-action dried yeast

1 teaspoon sugar

3 tablespoons olive oil

250 ml/1 cup lukewarm water

Topping

olive oil, for drizzling

several large pinches of sea salt flakes

100 g/⅔ cup cherry tomatoes

2 tablespoons Pesto (page 54), or store-bought fresh red or green pesto

a handful of fresh rosemary needles

1 red onion, thinly sliced

a baking sheet, dusted with flour

SERVES 6

You can use leftover risotto for these rice balls.
They can be prepared and rolled in advance; coat
them in breadcrumbs and fry just before serving.

mushroom & mozzarella
ARANCINI

1 tablespoon olive oil

2 tablespoons unsalted butter

2 shallots, finely chopped

1 garlic clove, crushed

15 g/½ oz. mushrooms, finely chopped

250 g/1¼ cups risotto rice (arborio or carnaroli)

750–850 ml/3–3½ cups vegetable stock

40 g/⅓ cup grated Italian-style hard cheese

1 tablespoon dried parsley or oregano

salt and black pepper

125 g/4 oz. mozzarella, diced

100 g/¾ cup plain/all-purpose flour

2 eggs, lightly beaten

200 g/2 cups breadcrumbs

1 litre/4 cups sunflower oil, for frying

Heat the olive oil and butter in a medium saucepan or pot set over a low–medium heat. Add the shallots, garlic and chopped mushrooms and cook until soft but not coloured. Add the rice to the pan and stir to coat well in the buttery mixture. Gradually add the vegetable stock, one ladleful at a time, and as it is absorbed by the rice, add another ladleful, stirring as you do so. Continue cooking in this way until the rice is **al dente** and the stock is used up. Remove the pan from the heat, add the grated cheese and herbs and season well with salt and black pepper. Tip the risotto into a bowl and set aside to cool completely.

Once the rice is cold, divide it into walnut-sized pieces and roll into balls. Taking one ball at a time, flatten it into a disc in the palm of your hand, press some diced mozzarella in the middle and wrap the rice around it to completely encase the cheese. Shape into a neat ball. Repeat with the remaining risotto.

Tip the flour, beaten eggs and breadcrumbs into separate shallow bowls. Roll the rice balls first in the flour, then coat well in the eggs and finally, roll them in the breadcrumbs to completely coat.

Fill a deep saucepan or pot with the sunflower oil to a depth of about 5 cm/2 inches. Heat until a cube of bread sizzles and browns in about 5 seconds. Cook the arancini, in batches, in the hot oil for 3–4 minutes or until crisp, hot and golden brown. Remove from the pan and drain on paper towels before serving.

MAKES 15–18

If you have a pestle and mortar it is a great stress-reliever bashing the herbs and cheese together. Alternatively, whizz everything together in a food processor for the same result.

homemade
PESTO

Peel the garlic and put it in a mortar or food processor with a small pinch of salt which will help to squash the garlic. Take the pestle and squash the garlic against the mortar.

Add the basil and bash the leaves, or pulse if you are using the food processor.

Then add the pine nuts and bash (or pulse) again. If you are using a pestle and mortar you will need to take it in turns with your roommates to help you bash everything together to stop your arm from aching! It will take a good few minutes.

Add the grated cheese and mix together just with a spoon.

Spoon the mixture into a bowl and gradually add the olive oil until the sauce just drops off your spoon. Hey presto! You've made pesto!

½ garlic clove

a pinch of salt

4 handfuls of fresh basil leaves

a big handful of pine nuts/kernels

2 handfuls of grated Italian-style hard cheese

about 2–3 tablespoons olive oil

MAKES ENOUGH FOR 2 SAUCEPANS OF PASTA

In Italy caponata is enjoyed as a warm vegetable side dish or as part of a cold antipasto. This classic Sicilian recipe is best enjoyed at room temperature as a dip with toasted ciabatta.

CAPONATA

1 aubergine/eggplant, cubed

salt and pepper

1 teaspoon cinnamon

2 tablespoons olive oil

1 red onion, chopped

2 celery stalks, sliced

1 garlic clove, crushed

1 x 400-g/14-oz. can chopped tomatoes

a handful of sultanas/golden raisins

2 tablespoons white wine

2 teaspoons capers, drained

1 tablespoon white wine vinegar

2 teaspoons sugar

a squeeze of fresh lemon juice, plus extra top serve

To serve

a handful of fresh flat-leaf parsley leaves, chopped

a drizzle of olive oil

slices of ciabatta, toasted

Season the aubergine/eggplant cubes generously with salt and pepper, and sprinkle with cinnamon.

Heat the olive oil in a large frying pan/skillet set over low heat, add the aubergine/eggplant and cook for about 10 minutes until soft and golden. Remove from the pan and set aside until needed.

Return the pan to the heat and add the onion, celery and garlic, and cook for about 8 minutes until the vegetables begin to soften. Add the tomatoes, sultanas/golden raisins and white wine, and simmer over low heat for 20 minutes.

Stir in the cooked aubergine/eggplant, add the capers, vinegar, sugar and lemon juice, and cook over low heat until the taste of vinegar softens. Remove from the heat and allow to cool to room temperature.

Finally, stir in the parsley and add a drizzle of olive oil and a squeeze of lemon juice. Spoon onto slices of toasted ciabatta and serve.

MAKES SUFFICIENT TOPPING FOR 16 SMALL TOASTS

BUON APPETITO

It's hard to beat a simple homemade risotto. Here tomatoes and sweet, liquoricy basil are stirred into buttery semi-cooked rice; the rice should be a little softened but still firm to the bite.

simple tomato & basil
RISOTTO

Pour the stock and wine in a medium saucepan or pot set over low heat.

Put half of the butter and the oil in a separate heavy-based saucepan or pot set over a medium heat. Add the garlic and leek and cook for 4–5 minutes, until softened. Add the rice and cook for 1 minute, until shiny and glossy.

Add about 65 ml/¼ cup of the hot stock mixture to the rice and stir constantly, until almost all of the liquid has been absorbed. Add another 65 ml/¼ cup to the pan, stirring until almost all the liquid has been absorbed. Continue adding the stock mixture a little at a time and stirring, until all the stock has been used and the rice is just tender.

Stir in the tomatoes, basil, grated cheese and remaining butter until well combined. Remove from the heat and transfer to warmed plates.

Drizzle with olive oil and serve immediately.

1 litre/4 cups vegetable stock

65 ml/¼ cup dry white wine

2 tablespoons butter

2 tablespoons olive oil, plus extra to drizzle

2 garlic cloves, chopped

1 large trimmed leek, sliced

325 g/1½ cups risotto rice (arborio or carnaroli)

3 fresh plum tomatoes, deseeded and finely diced

a large handful of fresh basil leaves, roughly torn

50 g/½ cup grated Italian-style hard cheese

SERVES 4

This mac 'n' cheese interpretation of a classic Italian dish is a guaranteed crowd pleaser, packed with flavour and pleasing to see.

aubergine
PARMIGIANA

500 g/1 lb. macaroni

4–5 tablespoons vegetable oil

1 large onion, finely chopped

1 teaspoon dried thyme

1 teaspoon dried oregano

1 teaspoon dried rosemary

3 garlic cloves, finely chopped

1 x 400-g/14-oz. can chopped tomatoes

1 medium aubergine/eggplant, sliced

1 x 470-g/16-oz. jar béchamel sauce

100 g/¾ cup grated Fontina

100 g/1¼ cups grated Italian-style hard cheese

125 g/1 cup shredded mozzarella

leaves from 2–3 sprigs fresh basil, coarsely torn

50 g/1 cup fresh breadcrumbs

salt and black pepper

SERVES 6–8

Bring a large saucepan or pot of salted water to the boil over a medium–high heat. Add the macaroni, stir well and cook according to the package instructions until very tender. Drain, rinse well let drip dry in a colander.

Preheat the oven to 200°C (400°F) Gas 6.

Heat 2 tablespoons of the oil in a large frying pan/skillet set over medium heat. Add the onion and cook for 5 minutes until just golden. Stir in the herbs and garlic and cook gently for 1 minute, then add the tomatoes and 1 teaspoon of salt and simmer gently for 20–30 minutes.

Arrange the aubergine/eggplant slices in a single layer on a baking sheet and drizzle over the remaining oil. Roast in the preheated oven for 15–20 minutes until tender. Remove from the oven, season and add to the tomatoes.

Preheat the grill/broiler to medium.

Warm the béchamel sauce in a small saucepan or pot set over a medium heat and add the grated cheeses, mixing well with a spoon to incorporate.

Put the cooked macaroni in a baking dish. Stir in the aubergine/eggplant mixture, pour over the hot béchamel sauce and mix well. Top with the mozzarella, the basil leaves and a good grinding of black pepper and sprinkle the breadcrumbs evenly over the top. Grill/broil for 5–10 minutes until the top is crunchy and golden brown.

Serve immediately.

Blissfully simple to make, with virtuous quantities of vegetables, this is a good way to eat well with very little effort. And you can use any vegetables you have to hand. Easy peasy!

BAKED RIGATONI
with mozzarella

Heat the oil in a large saucepan or pot set over a low heat. Add the onion and cook for 3–5 minutes, until soft. Add the carrot, celery and pepper. Season and cook for 2–3 minutes. Stir in the mushrooms and garlic and cook for 1 minute more. Add the wine and cook for 1 minute more. Stir in the chilli flakes, thyme, parsley, tomatoes, passata and sugar. Season generously and stir. Reduce the heat and simmer, uncovered, for 20–30 minutes.

Meanwhile, cook the pasta according to the packet instructions until **al dente**. Drain well and set aside.

Preheat the oven to 200°C (400°F) Gas 6.

Combine the cooked pasta and the vegetable sauce and mix well. Spread half the pasta in the prepared dish evenly. Top with half of the mozzarella, then the remaining pasta and arrange the remaining mozzarella slices on top.

Bake in the preheated oven for 25–30 minutes, until the cheese melts and bubbles.

Serve immediately.

SERVES 4–6

3 tablespoons olive oil

1 small onion, diced

1 carrot, finely diced

2–3 celery sticks, diced

1 small red, yellow or orange (bell) pepper, deseeded and diced

100 g/1½ cups mushrooms, diced

3 garlic cloves, finely chopped

125 ml/½ cup white or red wine

½–1 teaspoon dried red chilli flakes, to taste

1 teaspoon dried thyme

a large handful of fresh parsley or basil leaves, finely chopped

1 x 400-g/14-oz. can chopped tomatoes

1 x 700-g/24-oz. bottle passata (Italian sieved/strained tomatoes)

a pinch of sugar

500 g/1 lb. dried rigatoni

500 g/5 cups mozzarella, sliced

salt and black pepper

a 30 x 20-cm/ 12 x 8-inch baking dish, well oiled

The beauty of this recipe lies in its simplicity. It's a take on the traditional nut loaf turned into meatballs for an authentic vegetarian dish.

nutty
MEATBALLS

250 g/2½ cups mixed nuts (walnuts, cashews, almonds and chestnuts)

100 g/generous 1½ cups wholemeal/whole-wheat breadcrumbs

2 medium onions, peeled and quartered

1 celery stick

1 small carrot

2–3 garlic cloves, peeled

a small bunch of fresh flat-leaf parsley

3–5 tablespoons olive oil

1 teaspoon dried thyme

2 teaspoons vegetable stock powder

1 egg, beaten

1–2 tablespoons milk

salt and black pepper

To serve

1 x 500-g/17-oz. jar tomato sauce

cooked spaghetti or penne

finely grated Italian-style hard cheese

Preheat the oven to 180°C (350°F) Gas 4.

Put the nuts in the bowl of the food processor and pulse until finely ground. Add to the breadcrumbs, season lightly and set aside.

Put the onions, celery, carrot, garlic cloves and parsley in the food processor and pulse until finely chopped.

Heat 3 tablespoons of the oil in a large frying pan/skillet set over a medium heat. Add the onion mixture and thyme, and cook for 5–7 minutes, until softened. Remove from the heat and let cool slightly.

Add the cooked onion mixture to the nut mixture and stir well. Dissolve the stock powder in 125 ml/½ cup hot water and add to the onion mixture. Stir well. Add the egg and mix to combine. If the mixture is very dry, add the milk, or some water, 1 tablespoon at a time. The mixture needs to be soft or the finished dish will be dry.

Use your hands to shape the mixture into golf ball-size balls and arrange them on a baking sheet. Bake in the preheated oven for about 35 minutes, until browned.

Serve in warmed tomato sauce with pasta and finely grated cheese, if liked.

MAKES
4–6 SERVINGS

MAKES 6–8
SERVINGS

An indulgent supper dish that yields multiple portions that you can share with your housemates or freeze to eat another day.

veggie
LASAGNE

To make the vegetable bolognese, put the mushrooms, onion, carrot, leek, garlic and celery in a food processor and pulse until very finely chopped. Transfer to a frying pan/skillet set over a medium heat. Add the oil and thyme and cook for 3–5 minutes, stirring often, until just beginning to brown. Add the passata, tomatoes, sugar and bay leaf. Stir, then simmer, uncovered, for at least 15 minutes. Season to taste.

Preheat the oven to 200°C (400°F) Gas 6.

Put the ricotta, spinach, egg, grated Italian-style hard cheese and a good pinch each of salt and pepper in a mixing bowl and whisk until thoroughly blended.

Spread a thin layer of the vegetable bolognese in the bottom of the lasagne dish and drizzle with a little olive oil. Top with 2 sheets of lasagne. Spread with more of the bolognese and top with 2 more lasagne sheets. Spread half of the ricotta mixture on top and sprinkle with half the grated cheddar. Top with 2 lasagne sheets then spread with more bolognese. Top with 2 more lasagne sheets, spread over the remaining ricotta mixture and sprinkle over the remaining cheddar. Top with the remaining lasagne sheets and spread with a good layer of the bolognese.

Arrange the mozzarella slices on top and bake in the preheated oven for 30–40 minutes, until browned and bubbling.

Cut into portions and serve hot or transfer to an airtight container, let cool then freeze.

250-g/9-oz. tub ricotta

180 g/1½ cups chopped spinach

1 egg

4 tablespoons grated Italian-style hard cheese

1 x 300-g/10½-oz. lasagne sheets (minimum 10 slices)

80–100 g/½–1 cup grated vegetarian cheddar

2 x 125-g/4½-oz. balls mozzarella, sliced

salt and black pepper

Vegetable Bolognese

250 g/2½ cups chopped mushrooms

1 onion, coarsely chopped

1 carrot, coarsely chopped

1 small leek, washed

2 garlic cloves

1 celery stick, chopped

2–3 tablespoons olive oil

1 teaspoon dried thyme

700 ml/2¾ cups passata (Italian sieved/strained tomatoes)

1 x 400-g/14-oz. can chopped tomatoes

a pinch of sugar

1 dried bay leaf

a 20 x 25-cm/ 8 x 10-inch lasagne or baking dish

MIGHTY MEALS

Eggs can be thrown together in all manner of ways and with wonderful results. A frittata using whatever vegetables you happen to have is just one.

sweet potato & tomato
FRITTATA

Preheat the oven to 180°C (350°F) Gas 4.

Cut the potato in half lengthways and then into thin wedges. Toss in a roasting pan with 2 tablespoons olive oil and a little salt, pepper and dried chilli/red pepper flakes. Roast in the preheated oven for 20–25 minutes until just browned and starting to blister.

After 10 minutes, toss the red onions and tomatoes on a baking sheet with a few tablespoons of oil, the vinegar and a sprinkling of salt and place in the oven with the potato. The skins of the tomatoes should have just popped open and the red onions begun to caramelize when the sweet potato is ready to take out. Leave the oven on for the frittata.

Remove the cabbage leaves from their stalks and blanch in salted boiling water for about 2 minutes. Remove and refresh with cold water.

Crack the eggs into a bowl, whisk and season well.

Place the sweet potato, cabbage, tomatoes and onion (reserving some for on top) in the ovenproof frying pan/skillet or a quiche dish. Pour the beaten eggs over the top and finish with the reserved vegetables on top.

Cook in the still-warm oven for 25 minutes or until the frittata has puffed up and the top is just firm to the touch.

Meanwhile, combine the basil and garlic with 6 tablespoons olive oil to make a loose basil oil.

Allow the frittata to cool a little, then drizzle the basil oil over it and serve with a mixed leaf salad.

1 sweet potato

olive oil

salt and black pepper

dried chilli/hot red pepper flakes

2 red onions, sliced

a handful of ripe baby plum tomatoes

2 tablespoons balsamic vinegar

a bunch of cabbage leaves

10–12 eggs, depending on the size of your pan

Basil oil

a small bunch of fresh basil, finely chopped

1 garlic clove, crushed

20–25-cm/8–10-inch ovenproof frying pan/ skillet or quiche dish

With lentils it is all about the seasoning — oil, lemon juice and salt. Sun-dried tomatoes, lentils and aubergine/eggplant make the a wholesome main meal.

PUY LENTILS
with aubergine & sun-dried tomatoes

Wash and drain the lentils.

Heat 2 tablespoons oil in a large, heavy-bottomed, lidded casserole dish set over medium heat. Turn down the heat a little, add the onion and fry gently until soft and translucent but not coloured. Add the garlic and fry for 1 minute. Add the lentils and stir well. Pour the vegetable stock in and bring to the boil. Reduce the heat, simmer, then cover with the lid and cook for 25 minutes or until the lentils are tender and have absorbed most of the stock.

Meanwhile, heat a large, dry stovetop grill pan over medium heat until hot. Using a pastry brush, coat the aubergine/eggplant slices with oil on both sides. Place them on the hot pan and fry for a few minutes. Flip over and fry the other side for a few minutes until golden. Once cooked, they should be soft to the touch. Transfer to a plate and season with salt. Drizzle over the agave syrup and plenty of oil.

When the lentils are done, drain them of all but a few tablespoons of the cooking liquid. While they are still hot, season with the lemon zest and juice, vinegar and soy sauce and a few glugs of oil. Mix well and allow to cool slightly. Taste at room temperature and season if necessary. Add the tomatoes and mix together.

Combine the mint leaves with enough oil to make a dense mint oil.

To serve, nestle the aubergine/eggplant slices among the lentils, drizzle over the mint oil and scatter with the leaves.

300 g/1½ cups Puy lentils (or other green lentils)

olive oil

1 red onion, finely chopped

2 garlic cloves, crushed

450 ml/2 cups vegetable stock

3 aubergines/eggplants, topped, tailed and cut into ¼-cm/½-inch slices

salt and black pepper

grated zest of 1 lemon and juice of ½

100 g/⅔ cup sun-dried tomatoes

1 tablespoon runny honey

1 tablespoon red wine vinegar

1 tablespoon dark soy sauce

a big handful of fresh mint leaves, finely chopped, plus a few whole leaves to serve

SERVES 4.

Vibrant and lively in colour and taste these veggie burgers are perfect for a post-exam, celebratory summer BBQ. Just add sauce!

BEETROOT BURGERS

a handful of fresh dill

a handful of fresh parsley

leaves from 2 sprigs fresh thyme

350 g/11 oz. fresh beetroot/beets, grated

150 g/5 oz. carrot, finely grated

120 g/1 cup oatmeal

3 eggs

1 small red onion, finely chopped

2 garlic cloves, crushed

salt and black pepper

1 tablespoon vegetable oil

To serve

bread rolls

rocket/arugula

cherry tomatoes, halved

mustard

slaw

Preheat the oven to 180°C (350°F) Gas 4.

Finely chop the herbs. Thoroughly combine with the beetroot/beets, carrot, oatmeal, eggs, onion and garlic in a bowl, making sure the eggs and herbs are evenly distributed. Season with 1 teaspoon salt and a few grindings of pepper. Set aside for 15 minutes.

Form about 10 burger patties with your hands. Heat the vegetable oil in a frying pan/skillet set over a low heat and fry the burgers until just browned; 2–3 minutes on each side. Transfer to an ovenproof dish and bake in the preheated oven for 20 minutes.

Toast the bread rolls. Cut them open and spread with mustard on the inside. Add a little rocket/arugula and some halved tomatoes. Top with a cooked burger and a little slaw, and serve.

MAKES ABOUT 10

A fresh and colourful salad that is easy to prepare. Simply chop your preferred vegetables and roast them in the oven for 40 minutes.

ROASTED VEGETABLE SALAD
with grilled halloumi

Preheat the oven to 200°C (400°F) Gas 6.

Put all the vegetables in a large roasting pan with the olive oil and garlic cloves. Season well with salt and pepper and roast in the preheated oven for 40–60 minutes, until they are soft and golden but still holding their shape.

To make the basil oil, bring a small saucepan or pot of water to the boil over a medium–high heat. Put the basil leaves in the boiling water for just 10 seconds. Remove them and dip in a bowl of cold water. Drain and dry the basil leaves, then put them in a food processor and set the motor running. Drizzle in the olive oil then strain the mixture into a bowl and set aside.

Lightly oil a stovetop griddle/grill pan or frying pan/skillet and set over medium heat. Lay the strips of halloumi in the pan and cook until they turn golden brown, turning half way through cooking.

To assemble the salad, stir the rocket/arugula through the roasted vegetables. Peel the garlic cloves and add to the salad. Spoon the salad onto a serving plate and top with the halloumi. Drizzle with the basil oil and sprinkle over the pine nuts/kernels. Serve immediately.

2 red onions, peeled and quartered

1 aubergine/eggplant, cut into chunks

1 courgette/zucchini, cut into chunks

1 sweet potato, cut into chunks

1 red (bell) pepper, sliced into strips

a handful of cherry tomatoes

3 tablespoons olive oil

4 garlic cloves, unpeeled

250 g/9 oz. halloumi, sliced into strips

140 g/5 oz. rocket/arugula (about 2½ cups)

a small handful of toasted pine nuts/kernels

salt and black pepper

Basil oil

a small handful of basil leaves

100 ml/⅓ cup olive oil

SERVES 4

You can use pumpkin or sweet potato in place
of the squash here, or a combination of the two.
Serve with plenty of crusty bread.

SQUASH SALAD
with spiced lentils

275 g/1⅔ cups green lentils, rinsed and drained

50 g/½ cup walnut pieces

1 butternut squash, peeled, deseeded and cubed

3 tablespoons olive oil

1 large onion, halved and sliced

1 fresh red chilli, halved, deseeded and sliced

1 teaspoon ground cumin

1 teaspoon ground turmeric

1 teaspoon paprika

2 garlic cloves, crushed

1 x 400-g/14 oz. can chopped tomatoes

a pinch of sugar

a large handful of fresh flat-leaf parsley leaves, chopped

a small handful of fresh coriander/cilantro leaves, finely chopped

freshly squeezed juice of ½ a lemon

250 g/1 cup feta, crumbled

salt and black pepper

SERVES 4

Preheat the oven to 190°C (375°F) Gas 5.

Put the lentils in a saucepan or pot with sufficient cold water to cover. Add a pinch of salt, bring to the boil over a medium–high heat, then reduce the heat and simmer for 20–30 minutes, until tender. Drain and set aside.

Dry roast the walnuts in a small frying pan/skillet set over a low heat, until browned. Set aside.

Arrange the squash cubes on a baking sheet, toss with 2 tablespoons of the oil and sprinkle with a little salt. Roast in the preheated oven for 30–35 minutes, until tender, turning halfway through cooking time.

Heat the remaining oil in a large saucepan or pot set over a low heat. Add the onion and cook for 3–5 minutes, until soft. Add the chilli, cumin, turmeric, paprika, garlic and a pinch of salt and cook, stirring for 1 minute. Add the tomatoes, sugar, another pinch of salt, half the parsley and half the coriander/cilantro. Simmer, uncovered, for 20 minutes, stirring in the cooked lentils about 5 minutes before the end of cooking time, just to warm through. Taste and adjust the seasoning if necessary.

Add the roasted squash, the remaining herbs and a squeeze of lemon juice. Taste and adjust the seasoning. Crumble over the feta, add the walnuts and serve immediately with plenty of crusty bread.

This recipe is a 'stone soup' formula for using up a little bit of this, and a little bit of that all based around a single spud and a few veggie sausages. A true super-cheap and super-tasty supper!

VEGGIE SAUSAGE
casserole

Heat 2 tablespoons of the oil in a large deep frying pan/skillet with a lid set over a low heat. Add the onion and pepper and cook for 3–5 minutes, until just soft. Add the mushrooms, thyme, chilli/hot pepper flakes (if using) and the remaining oil and cook for a further 3–5 minutes, until the mushrooms begin to brown.

Add the sausages and cook until they begin to brown. Stir in the garlic and potato and cook for 1 minute more, stirring. Season lightly. Add the lentils and pasta sauce and stir well. You may need to add some water; the mixture should almost cover the potato pieces. Reduce the heat, cover with a lid, and simmer gently for about 30 minutes, until the potatoes are tender.

Remove the lid and simmer for 3–5 minutes to reduce the liquid a bit more. Sprinkle with finely chopped fresh herbs and serve immediately.

4 tablespoons olive oil

1 onion, diced

1 yellow (bell) pepper, diced

150 g/1½ cups coarsely chopped mushrooms

½ teaspoon dried thyme

a pinch of dried chilli/hot pepper flakes (optional)

2–4 vegetarian sausages, sliced

1–2 garlic cloves, crushed

1 large waxy potato, diced

1 x 400-g/14-oz. can cooked lentils, drained and rinsed

1 x 400-g/14-oz. jar any tomato pasta sauce

salt and black pepper

finely chopped fresh herbs, to serve

MAKES 4 SERVINGS

The amount of cooked barley required for this recipe is half the amount shown, but the remaining half can be frozen, making it really quick to prepare this soup again in the future.

vegetable & barley
SOUP

1–2 tablespoons olive oil

1 small onion, finely chopped

1 small leek, halved and thinly sliced

1 carrot, quartered lengthwise and thinly sliced

1 celery stick, halved lengthwise and thinly sliced

1¼ litres/5 cups vegetable stock

100 g/½ cup barley, cooked according to package instructions and drained

salt and black pepper

Heat the oil in a large saucepan or pot set over a medium heat. Add the onion, leek, carrot and celery and cook for about 5 minutes, until just soft.

Season lightly, depending upon the salt content of your stock. If in doubt, season gradually and taste frequently. Add the stock, bring just to the boil, then reduce the heat, cover and simmer gently for at least 15 minutes, until the vegetables are tender.

Stir in half of the barley and taste for seasoning. Add more water or stock if the soup is too thick.

Serve hot or let cool before transferring to an airtight container and store in the fridge until you are ready to eat.

MAKES 4–6 SERVINGS

Tofu is not something that is eaten much in Mexico
but it is very healthy and its unique texture adds
another dimension to this dish. It also combines
very well with a bit of heat.

TOFU TACOS

First, prepare the ingredients. Cut the tofu into strips about 5 cm/2 inches long. Cut the onion and (bell) peppers into strips and thinly slice the garlic and Jalapeño.

Melt the butter in a frying pan/skillet set over high heat, then fry the tofu for about 5 minutes.

Add the onion, (bell) peppers, garlic, oregano, salt and pepper and fry for 5 minutes.

The tofu should be brown and a little crispy at the edges and the peppers should still have a little crunch.

Stir in the chopped Jalapeño.

Place a dry frying pan/skillet over high heat. Warm each tortilla for about 20–30 seconds on each side. Then, spoon the ingredients over the tortillas and serve with a mild tomato salsa.

400 g/14 oz. tofu

½ red onion

1 red (bell) pepper

1 yellow (bell) pepper

2 garlic cloves

1 fresh Jalapeño (or a couple of Thai green chillies for more heat)

20 g/1½ tablespoons butter

½ teaspoon dried oregano

¼ teaspoon salt

¼ teaspoon ground white pepper

To serve

8 x 15-cm/6-in. corn or flour tortillas

mild tomato salsa

SERVES 4

POT LUCK

SERVES 4

This stew is packed with root vegetables making it both hearty and healthy. It's also very versatile so use whatever vegetables you have to hand. Fresh peas and asparagus are delicious in summer.

WINTER VEGETABLE STEW
with herbed dumplings

Preheat the oven to 180°C (350°F) Gas 4.

Put the oil and butter in a casserole dish set over a medium heat. Add the shallots and cook for 2 minutes. Add the potatoes, parsnip, carrots, mushrooms and leek and cook for 5 minutes, stirring occasionally, until the vegetables start to turn golden. Reduce the heat slightly and add the garlic and thyme. Season generously with salt and pepper, then stir in the mustard. Add the flour and stir until the vegetables are well coated and the flour has disappeared. Add the vinegar and wine and cook for 2 minutes. Add the butter beans and beetroot/beets, stir gently, then add the vegetable stock.

Bring the mixture to the boil and boil for 2 minutes. Then cover with a lid and transfer to the oven. Bake for 40–50 minutes.

Meanwhile, prepare the dumplings. Sift the flour and baking powder into a bowl. Rub the cold butter into the flour. When the mixture looks like breadcrumbs and there are no lumps of butter, stir in the chopped herbs and season with salt and pepper. Add a couple of tablespoons of water, or enough to bring the mixture together to form a stiff dough.

Divide the dough into walnut-size balls. Cover with clingfilm/plastic wrap and chill in the fridge until the stew is cooked. When the stew is ready, put the dumplings on the top of the stew so that they are half submerged. Cover with a lid and return the stew to the oven and cook for 20 minutes until the dumplings have puffed up and are golden on the top.

2 tablespoons each olive oil and butter

3 shallots, quartered

2 white potatoes, cut into chunks

1 parsnip, cut into chunks

250 g/9 oz. baby carrots

250 g/4 cups mushrooms

1 leek, sliced into rings

2 garlic cloves, crushed

4 sprigs fresh thyme

1 teaspoon mustard

2 tablespoons plain/all-purpose flour

1 tablespoon balsamic vinegar

240 ml/1 cup white wine

1 x 400-g/14-oz. can butter beans

250 g/9 oz. fresh raw beetroot/beets, peeled and cut into chunks

300 ml/1¼ cups vegetable stock

salt and black pepper

For the herbed dumplings

250 g/2 cups plain/all-purpose flour

2 teaspoons baking powder

125 g/1 stick salted butter, chilled

a handful of fresh herbs

This simple, light and healthy curry is easy to make and does not require an extensive stock of spices. Serve it with a generous spoonful of plain yogurt and some steamed rice.

roasted aubergine, sweet potato & spinach
CURRY

Preheat the oven to 180°C (350°F) Gas 4.

Put the aubergine/eggplant and sweet potato on a baking sheet and season with salt and pepper. Drizzle with the olive oil and sprinkle with cinnamon. Roast in the preheated oven for about 40 minutes, until cooked and golden.

Heat the vegetable oil in a large saucepan or pot set over a medium heat. When the oil is hot, add the mustard seeds and cover with a lid. Cook for 2 minutes or until they pop. Reduce the heat, uncover, and add the shallot, ginger, garlic, and chilli/chile. Fry for 3 minutes until they start to soften. Add the garam masala and sugar and fry for 5 minutes. Finally, add the tomatoes and simmer for 15 minutes.

Stir the roasted vegetables through the sauce and cook over a low heat for about 10 minutes, then stir in the spinach until wilted. Taste and adjust the seasoning by adding more sugar, lime or salt and pepper, to taste.

Spoon onto serving plates and serve hot with rice.

2 aubergines/eggplants, chopped into bite-size pieces

1 sweet potato, peeled and chopped into bite-size pieces

2 tablespoons olive oil

1 tablespoon ground cinnamon

1 tablespoon vegetable oil

½ teaspoon mustard seeds

1 shallot, chopped

2-cm/¾-inch piece of fresh ginger, peeled and grated

2 garlic cloves, crushed

1 fresh red chilli/chile, finely chopped

2 teaspoons garam masala

2 teaspoons sugar

1 x 400-g/14-oz. can chopped tomatoes

a large handful of fresh spinach, washed and dried

a pinch of sugar, to taste

a squeeze of fresh lime juice

salt and black pepper

a handful of fresh coriander/cilantro leaves, finely chopped

cooked rice, to serve

SERVES 4–6

This technique of cooking rice is Middle Eastern in origin but has spread far and wide — similar rice dishes can be found in European, Asian, Latin American, Caribbean and Indian cuisines.

orange veg & spring onion
PILAU

2 tablespoons light olive oil

1 onion, chopped

2 garlic cloves, chopped

1 teaspoon ground ginger

1 large red chilli/chile, finely chopped

1 teaspoon ground coriander

1 teaspoon ground cumin

1 teaspoon turmeric

50 g/⅔ cup flaked/slivered almonds

300 g/3¼ cups basmati rice

1 carrot, cut into large chunks

200 g/ pumpkin or squash, peeled, deseeded and cut into wedges

1 small sweet potato, peeled and cut into thick half-circles

freshly squeezed juice of 1 lime

a handful of fresh coriander/cilantro leaves, chopped

Put the oil in a heavy-based saucepan or pot set over a high heat. Add the onion, garlic, ginger and chilli and cook for 5 minutes, stirring often. Add the spices and almonds and cook for a further 5 minutes, until the spices become aromatic and look very dark in the pan.

Add the rice and cook for a minute, stirring well to coat the rice in the spices. Add the carrot, pumpkin and sweet potato to the pan. Pour in 600 ml/2 cups water and stir well, loosening any grains of rice that are stuck to the bottom of the pan. Bring to the boil, then reduce the heat, cover with a tight-fitting lid and cook for 25 minutes, stirring occasionally.

Add the lime juice and coriander/cilantro, stir well to combine and serve hot.

SERVES 4

This stew is named Napolitana because of the predominance of tomatoes in this Mediterranean-style stew although the flavours could easily be described as Greek, with fresh oregano and feta.

napolitana
LENTIL STEW

Put the lentils in a large saucepan or pot set over a high heat. Add sufficient cold water to cover and bring to the boil, then reduce the heat and let simmer for 20 minutes until the lentils are tender but retain a little bite. Drain and set aside.

Put the oil in a saucepan or pot set over a high heat. Add the onion, garlic, oregano and chilli/hot pepper flakes and cook for 5 minutes, stirring often, until the onion softens. Add the capers, tomatoes, passata, lentils and 250 ml/1 cup water. Bring to the boil, then reduce the heat and let simmer gently for 10 minutes, stirring occasionally.

Spoon into warmed serving dishes, top with the olives and crumbled feta and serve with crusty bread on the side for dipping into the rich sauce.

100 g/½ cup green or brown lentils

3 tablespoons olive oil

1 onion, chopped

2 garlic cloves, chopped

2 teaspoons dried oregano

1 teaspoon dried chilli/hot pepper flakes

1½ tablespoons salted capers, rinsed

2 ripe tomatoes, roughly chopped

250 g/9 oz. passata (Italian sieved/strained tomatoes)

60 g/⅔ cup small black olives

100 g/½ cup feta cheese, crumbled

crusty bread, to serve

SERVES 4

This is a hearty hotpot packed with vegetables and rich with smoky paprika. Butter beans are large and white with a delicate flavour that complements the stronger flavours of garlic and paprika.

SMOKY BEAN HOTPOT

100 g/½ cup dried large butter beans

2 tablespoons olive oil

1 large onion, chopped

2 garlic cloves, chopped

2 teaspoons smoked paprika

1 celery stick, chopped

1 carrot, chopped

2 medium waxy potatoes, cut into 2-cm/¾-inch dice

1 red pepper, chopped

500 ml/2 cups vegetable stock

salt and black pepper

crusty bread, to serve

Soak the dried beans in cold water for at least 6 hours or overnight. Drain and put in a large saucepan or pot set over a medium heat, with sufficient just-boiled water to cover. Cook for 30 minutes until softened. Drain and set aside until needed.

Put the oil in a saucepan or pot set over a medium heat. Add the onion and cook for 4–5 minutes until softened. Add the garlic and paprika and stir-fry for 2 minutes. Then add the celery, carrot, potatoes and red pepper and cook for 2 minutes, stirring constantly to coat the vegetables in the flavoured oil.

Pour in the stock and beans and bring to the boil. Reduce the heat and partially cover the pan with a lid. Let simmer for 40 minutes, stirring often, until all the vegetables are cooked.

Season to taste and serve with crusty bread.

SERVES 4

This falls somewhere between a stew and a soup.
Make use of the abundant sauce and serve with
fragrant jasmine rice. If you like things spicy,
add two chillies and all their seeds; if not,
use one and keep the seeds out.

aromatic
THAI CURRY

Heat the oil in a large saucepan or pot set over a low heat.
Add the onion and cook for 3–5 minutes, until just soft. Add
the ginger, chillies/chiles, curry powder, cumin and a pinch
of salt. Cook for 1–2 minutes, stirring, until aromatic.

Add the sweet potatoes and stir to coat in the spices. Add
the coconut milk and stock and a little water if necessary,
just to cover the sweet potatoes; the mixture should be
soupy as it will cook down. Bring to the boil, then simmer,
uncovered, for 15 minutes.

Add the chickpeas and continue to simmer for 15–20 minutes
longer, until the sweet potatoes are tender.

Add the spinach, in batches, stirring to blend and waiting
for each batch to wilt before adding the next.

Serve immediately with jasmine rice.

1 tablespoon vegetable oil

1 onion, halved and sliced

a 4-cm/1½-inch piece of fresh
ginger, peeled and finely chopped
or grated

1–2 fresh red chillies/chiles,
halved and sliced

1 teaspoon curry powder

1 teaspoon ground cumin

1.3 kg/3-lbs. sweet potatoes,
peeled and cubed

1 x 400-ml/14-oz. can coconut
milk

450 ml/scant 2 cups vegetable
stock

1 x 400-g/14-oz. can chickpeas,
drained

225 g/4 cups baby spinach leaves

salt

jasmine rice, to serve

SERVES 4

This is a light, summery stew and is best eaten lukewarm or at room temperature with a glass of wine or fresh grapefruit juice. Serve with toasted pitta bread and wedges of fresh lemon to squeeze.

Greek summer vegetable
STEW

2 tablespoons olive oil

1 onion, chopped

450 g/1 lb. small new potatoes, cubed

330 g/12 oz. courgette/zucchini, halved and quartered lengthwise, then sliced thickly

3 garlic cloves, sliced

¼ teaspoon paprika

¼ teaspoon cayenne pepper

2 x 400 g/14-oz. cans chopped tomatoes

a small bunch of flat-leaf parsley, finely chopped

a small bunch of dill, finely chopped

250 g/9 oz. haricot verts/fine green beans, halved

100 g/¾ cup green olives, pitted

freshly squeezed juice of ½ a lemon

salt and black pepper

Heat the oil in a large saucepan or pot set over a low heat. Add the onion and cook for 3–5 minutes, until soft. Add the potatoes, courgette/zucchini, garlic, paprika, cayenne, and a pinch of salt and cook, stirring to coat in the oil, for 1 minute.

Add the tomatoes, parsley, and some of the dill. Stir to combine and add some water to thin slightly; about 125 ml/½ cup should be enough. Season well, then cover and simmer for 30 minutes.

Add the haricot verts/green beans, cover, and continue to simmer for about 20 minutes longer, until the beans are tender.

Stir in the olives, lemon juice, and remaining dill.

Serve at room temperature with pitta bread.

SERVES 4–6

Microwave the aubergines/eggplant to pre-cook them and keep oil absorption to a minimum. If you don't have a microwave, light steaming will have the same effect. Serve with rice and a little grated cheese to make a complete meal.

RATATOUILLE

Put the aubergine/eggplant cubes in a microwave-proof bowl with 3 tablespoons water and microwave on high for 6 minutes. Drain and set aside.

Heat 3 tablespoons of the oil in a large saucepan or pot set over a low heat. Add the onions and cook for 3–5 minutes, until soft. Season with a little salt.

Add the (bell) peppers and cook for a further 5–8 minutes, stirring occasionally. Season with a little salt.

Add 1 more tablespoon of the oil and then the courgettes/zucchini. Mix well and cook for 5 minutes longer. Season with a little more salt.

Add 2 more tablespoons of the oil and the drained aubergines/eggplant. Cook, stirring often, for 5 minutes. Add the tomatoes, 5 of the garlic cloves, half of the basil and 1 more tablespoon of the oil, if required. Check the seasoning and adjust if necessary. Cook for 5 minutes. Cover, reduce the heat and simmer gently for 30 minutes, stirring occasionally.

Stir in the remaining garlic and basil just before serving.

Serve with rice or crusty bread, as preferred.

1 kg/2 lbs. 2 oz. aubergines/eggplant, cut into cubes

6–7 tablespoons olive oil

2 onions, coarsely chopped

2 red (bell) peppers, halved, deseeded and cut into pieces

2 yellow (bell) peppers, halved, deseeded and cut into pieces

1 green (bell) pepper, halved, deseeded and cut into pieces

750 g/1 lb. 8 oz. courgettes/zucchini, halved lengthways and sliced

6 fresh plum tomatoes, halved, deseeded and chopped

6 garlic cloves, crushed

a large handful of fresh basil leaves, coarsely chopped

salt and black pepper

rice or crusty bread, to serve (optional)

SERVES 4–6

This syrupy, caramelized tagine is delicious served as a main dish, with couscous. Sweet potatoes, butternut squash, and pumpkin can be used instead of true yams.

carrot, shallot & prune
TAGINE

2–3 tablespoons olive oil with a knob/pat of butter

a 4-cm/1½-inch piece of fresh ginger, peeled and finely chopped or grated

1–2 teaspoons ground cinnamon

about 16 small shallots, peeled and left whole

16 oz./1¾ lb. yam, peeled and cut into bite-size chunks

2 medium carrots, peeled and cut into bite-size chunks

75 g/¾ cup pitted prunes

1 tablespoon runny honey

500 ml/2 cups vegetable stock

a small bunch of coriander/cilantro leaves, roughly chopped

a few fresh mint leaves, chopped

salt and black pepper

Heat the olive oil and butter in a tagine or heavy-based casserole dish set over a medium–high heat. Stir in the ginger and cinnamon. Toss in the shallots and when they begin to color add the yam and the carrots. Sauté for 2–3 minutes, then add the prunes and the honey.

Pour in the stock and bring it to a boil. Reduce the heat, cover with a lid, and cook gently for about 25 minutes.

Remove the lid and stir in some of the coriander/cilantro and mint. Season to taste with salt and pepper and reduce the liquid, if necessary, by cooking for a further 2–3 minutes without the lid.

The vegetables should be tender and slightly caramelized in a very syrupy sauce. Sprinkle with the remaining coriander/cilantro and mint and serve immediately.

SERVES 4–6

WOW CHOW

These tasty dumplings make an impressive sharing plate or appetizer — they can be made ahead of time and frozen.

DUMPLINGS
with dipping sauce

To make the dumplings, heat the sesame oil in a frying pan/skillet set over a medium–high heat and add the mushrooms, pak choi/bok choy and carrot. Cook for 5 minutes.

Put the cooked mushrooms, pak choi/bok choy and carrots in a food processor along with the spring onions/scallions, garlic, chilli/chile, ginger and coriander/cilantro and blitz. Alternatively, finely chop all of the ingredients by hand.

Dust the work surface with a little cornflour/cornstarch and put the dumpling wrappers on the floured surface. Put 1 teaspoon of the filling in the centre of each wrapper. Using a pastry brush, moisten the edges of each wrapper with a little water, then seal the edges together starting at the centre and ensuring there is no air trapped in the wrapper. Make sure that the dumpling is well sealed – if not, add a little more water to seal it. You can use your finger to frill the edge of the dumpling for decoration.

Put a colander over a pan of boiling water. Place a sheet of baking parchment inside the colander and put the dumplings inside. Cover with a lid and steam for 10–15 minutes until the filling is hot and cooked.

For extra flavour and texture, once the dumplings have been steamed, heat a tablespoon of sesame oil in a frying pan/skillet over a high heat and fry the dumplings for 1–2 minutes, until the bottom and sides start to colour.

To make the dipping sauce, put all of the ingredients in a small bowl and stir until well combined.

The uncooked dumplings will keep covered in the fridge for a few hours. Alternatively, steam the dumplings, let them cool, then store them, well wrapped, in the fridge for a few hours.

1 tablespoon sesame oil, plus extra for frying

120 g/4 oz. Shitake mushrooms

1 pak choi/bok choy

1 carrot, grated

6 spring onions/scallions, finely sliced

2 garlic cloves

1–2 fresh red chillis/chiles

a 2-cm/¾-inch piece of fresh ginger, peeled and finely chopped or grated

a handful of fresh coriander/cilantro

1 pack of frozen round dumpling (gyoza) wrappers or wonton wrappers, defrosted

cornflour/cornstarch, for dusting

Dipping sauce

3 tablespoons dark soy sauce

2 teaspoons dark brown sugar

1 tablespoon sesame oil

2 tablespoons rice vinegar

1 garlic clove, crushed

1 teaspoon finely grated fresh ginger

½–1 fresh red chilli/chile, very finely chopped

a squeeze of fresh lemon juice

a handful of fresh coriander/cilantro, chopped

MAKES 18

SERVES 4

Home-made enchiladas are so much easier to make than you think and so very delicious.

ENCHILADAS

Preheat the oven to 200°C (400°F) Gas 6.

To make the sauce, put the onion and garlic in a food processor and pulse until finely chopped. Transfer to a large frying pan/skillet. Add the oil and cook over low heat, stirring, for 3–5 minutes, until just soft. Stir in the chilli/hot pepper flakes, paprika, cumin and oregano and add salt to taste. Cook, stirring, for 2 minutes. Add the passata and stock and simmer gently, uncovered, for at least 15 minutes. Let cool slightly.

Meanwhile, make the filling. Heat the oil in a large saucepan or pot set over a low heat, add the courgettes and onion and cook for 5–8 minutes, until just tender. Stir in the sweetcorn, chilli, cumin and beans and season to taste. Remove from the heat and stir in the coriander/cilantro.

To assemble, warm the tortillas according to the packet instructions. Coat the bottom of a baking dish with a layer of the tomato sauce. Working one at a time, dab a tortilla gently in the warm sauce in the pan, just to coat the bottom side, then turn over to coat the other side.

Transfer the coated tortilla to a plate and fill with a large spoonful of filling, a handful of grated cheese, then fold the tortilla over to enclose the filling and transfer it in a baking dish, seam-side down. Continue until all the tortillas have been filled. Spoon the remaining sauce over the tortillas, concentrating on the ends as these tend to dry out. Sprinkle the remaining cheese down the centre.

Bake in the preheated oven for 15–20 minutes, until the cheese has melted. Sprinkle with more coriander/cilantro and serve with soured cream on the side.

2 tablespoons olive oil

450 g/16 oz. courgettes/zucchini, diced

1 red onion, diced

150 g/1 cup sweetcorn kernels

½ fresh red or green chilli, halved, deseeded and sliced

1 teaspoon ground cumin

1 x 400-g/14-oz. can black beans, drained

a handful of fresh coriander/cilantro leaves, chopped

8 corn tortillas

250 g/2½ cups vegetarian cheddar, grated

soured cream, to serve

Spicy tomato sauce

1 onion, coarsely chopped

2 garlic cloves

2 tablespoons olive oil

1–2 teaspoons dried red chilli/hot pepper flakes, to taste

½ teaspoon hot smoked paprika

1 teaspoon ground cumin

1 teaspoon dried oregano

1 x 700-g/25-oz. jar passata (Italian sieved/strained tomatoes)

375 ml/1½ cups vegetable stock

salt and black pepper

These light, fresh-tasting corncakes are ideal
served as a canapé with drinks. They also make
a great brunch dish if the corncakes are bigger.

CORNCAKES
with spicy avocado salsa

225 g/1½ cups plus 1 tablespoon
plain/all-purpose flour

1½ teaspoons baking powder

½ teaspoon salt

30 g/2 tablespoons butter

225 ml/1 cup milk

1 egg, lightly beaten

160 g/1 heaped cup canned or
frozen sweetcorn

½–1 fresh red chilli/chile, finely
chopped or 1 teaspoon chilli/
hot red pepper flakes

a small handful of fresh
coriander/cilantro, finely chopped

Spicy avocado salsa

2 avocados, pitted

2 tablespoons freshly chopped
coriander/cilantro, chopped

2 small shallots, finely chopped

1–2 fresh red chillies/chiles,
finely chopped

freshly grated zest of 2 limes

2 tablespoons freshly squeezed
lime juice

a pinch of sugar

salt and black pepper

To make the spicy avocado salsa, half chop, half mash the
avocado (depending on its ripeness) with the herbs and
shallots in a bowl to combine. Add the remaining
ingredients, season well with salt and pepper, using a
little more lime juice, chilli/chile or sugar, if needed.

For the corncakes, sift the flour into a mixing bowl and
add the baking powder and salt. Set aside.

Melt the butter in a small saucepan or pot set over a
low heat. In a separate bowl combine the milk, egg,
sweetcorn, chilli/chile and coriander/cilantro. Add the
melted butter and stir to combine.

Make a well in the centre of the dry ingredients. Pour in
the wet ingredients and stir from the centre to gradually
mix them together so that there are no lumps. Set aside
for 10 minutes.

Lightly grease a frying pan/skillet and let it heat up over
a medium–high heat. Put teaspoons of the mixture into
the pan (it will spread a little). Cook until the pancakes
are golden brown, turning over halfway through.

To serve, top with a spoonful of spicy avocado salsa.

MAKES 24

This crunchy salad is perfect as an appetizer to serve as part of an Asian meal. You can use any fresh vegetables that you have to hand.

HOT & SOUR SALAD
with marinated tofu

For the marinated tofu, put all of the ingredients except the tofu in a bowl and stir until well combined. Put the tofu in a separate bowl, pour the marinade over it and set aside to marinate for 30 minutes.

Bring a saucepan of water to the boil and cook the asparagus and mange tout/snow peas for 3 minutes, until they soften slightly but still have a crunch to them. Remove them from the boiling water and put them into a bowl of ice-cold water to stop the cooking process. Drain, then slice in half lengthways and put them in a serving bowl. Add the cashews to the serving bowl.

Put all of the dressing ingredients in a bowl and stir until well combined. Place the rest of the salad ingredients in the serving bowl, add the dressing and toss to coat the salad. Crumble the marinated tofu over the salad and finish with a sprinkling of sesame seeds.

SERVES 4

100 g/about 1 cup asparagus tips

100 g/about 1 cup mange tout/snow peas

50 g/⅓ cup toasted cashews

100 g/2 cup fresh beansprouts

1 carrot, sliced into ribbons

1 tablespoon toasted sesame seeds, to serve

Marinated tofu

200 g/7 oz. tofu

2 tablespoons sesame oil

1 tablespoon dark soy sauce

½ fresh red chilli/chile, finely chopped

1 teaspoon grated fresh ginger

grated zest and freshly squeezed juice of ½ a lime

½ teaspoon sugar

Dressing

½ teaspoon salt

2 teaspoons sugar

grated zest and freshly squeezed juice of 1 lime

1 teaspoon white wine vinegar

½ fresh red chilli/chile

Packed with flavour, this dish makes a welcome change from lasagne and is always a crowd pleaser.

vegetable & lentil
MOUSSAKA

2 aubergines/eggplants, sliced lengthways

5 tablespoons olive oil

1 red onion, finely chopped

120 ml/½ cup white wine

1 carrot, finely chopped

1 red bell pepper, finely chopped

½ courgette/zucchini, finely chopped

a handful of dill, finely chopped

1 teaspoon dried oregano

1 teaspoon ground cinnamon

100 g/½ cup red lentils

1 x 400-g/14-oz. can chopped plum tomatoes

600 g/1 lb 5 oz. potatoes, peeled and sliced

400 g/about 2 cups plain yogurt

2 eggs

zest of 1 unwaxed lemon

freshly grated nutmeg

60 g/½ cup crumbled feta cheese

salt and black pepper

SERVES 4

Preheat the oven to 180°C (350°F) Gas 4.

Sprinkle the aubergine/eggplants with salt and 2 tablespoons olive oil and bake in the preheated oven for 15–20 minutes, until soft and starting to brown.

Meanwhile, put the onion in a large saucepan or pot set over a low heat with 1 tablespoon olive oil and 1 tablespoon water. Cover and cook for 5–10 minutes until the onion softens without taking on any colour. Take off the lid, add the wine and boil over high heat until the wine has reduced by half. Add the carrot, bell pepper, courgette/zucchini, dill, oregano, and cinnamon and fry until they turn golden brown. Add the lentils and tomatoes, along with 240 ml/1 cup of water and simmer over low heat for 20 minutes. Season with salt and pepper, to taste.

Fry the potatoes in the remaining 2 tablespoons olive oil until they are golden on either side and the potato has started to soften. Remove from the pan and set aside.

To assemble the moussaka, lay half of the aubergine/eggplant on the bottom of an ovenproof dish, cover with half of the lentil mixture and top with half of the potatoes. Repeat until you have used all the ingredients.

To make the topping, whisk the yogurt with the eggs, lemon, nutmeg and half of the feta. Pour on top of the moussaka and sprinkle the top with the remaining crumbled feta. Bake in the oven for 45 minutes until the top is golden brown.

Serve hot or at room temperature.

110

Samosas are easier to make than they look. Traditionally deep-fried, they can also be baked, as here.

SAMOSAS

To make the filling, cube the courgette/zucchini and remove excess liquid following the instructions given on page 130. Chop the sundried tomatoes and feta put in a bowl with the lemon zest, garlic, chilli/hot red pepper flakes, mustard seeds and nutmeg. Combine well and season to taste with salt and pepper. Set aside until ready to fill the samosas.

To make the yogurt dip, combine the yogurt, lemon zest and garlic in a bowl. Season to taste with lemon juice, salt and pepper.

Preheat oven to 200°C (400°F) Gas 6.

To make the samosas, melt the butter in a small saucepan or pot set over low heat. Brush one sheet of pastry dough with melted butter, then lay another pastry sheet on top (giving you 2 layers of filo/phyllo). Cut each layered sheet into 3 strips. Lightly brush with butter. (Keep the remaining pastry well covered under a damp kitchen towel until needed.) Put a tablespoon of filling at one end of a strip leaving a 1-cm/ ³⁄₈-inch gap at the bottom and on either side. Form the filling into a rough triangle, and fold the bottom excess up onto the filling. Roll the samosa up tightly, making the shape of the triangle. Brush with butter and sprinkle with poppy or sesame seeds, and put on a lined baking sheet. Repeat with the remaining pastry.

Bake in the preheated oven for 10–12 minutes until the samosas are golden brown, and serve immediately, with lemon and garlic yogurt dip.

100 g/½ cup minus 1 tablespoon butter

12 sheets of filo/phyllo pastry

2 tablespoons poppy seeds

Filling

2 courgettes/zucchini, deseeded

120 g/1 cup sundried tomatoes

200 g/7 oz. feta

finely grated zest of 1 lemon

1 garlic clove, crushed

½ teaspoon chilli/hot red pepper flakes

1 teaspoon mustard seeds

½ teaspoon ground nutmeg

salt and black pepper

Lemon & garlic yogurt dip

300 ml/about 1½ cups plain yogurt

grated zest and juice of 2 lemons

2 garlic cloves, crushed

salt and black pepper

MAKES 18

Make the mushrooms on their own and serve them as an appetizer or light lunch, or add the creamy, mustard beans to make a warming supper dish.

STUFFED MUSHROOMS
with creamy white beans

2 garlic cloves, crushed

4 tablespoons olive oil

4 tablespoons white wine

leaves from a sprig of rosemary

4 large portobello mushrooms, peeled, with stalks removed and reserved for the filling

1 tablespoon capers, drained and chopped

a handful of chopped flat-leaf parsley leaves

4 tablespoons/¼ cup breadcrumbs

olive oil, for brushing

salt and black pepper

Creamy white beans

½ white onion, finely chopped

30 g/2 tablespoons butter

1 x 400-g/14-oz. can butter/lima beans, drained

150 ml/⅔ cup vegetable stock

2 teaspoons Dijon mustard

3 tablespoons single/light cream (optional)

a handful of spinach, finely chopped

salt and black pepper

Preheat the oven to 180°C (350°F) Gas 4.

To make the mushrooms, combine the garlic, oil, wine and rosemary together in a bowl. Pour this over the mushrooms and leave them to marinate for 30 minutes.

To make the stuffing for the mushrooms, chop the mushroom stalks and combine them with the capers, parsley, breadcrumbs, salt and pepper in a bowl and add 1 tablespoon of the marinade. Spoon the stuffing on top of the mushrooms, gills-side up.

Put the mushrooms in an ovenproof dish and bake in the preheated oven for 15 minutes.

To make the beans, put the onion in a saucepan with the butter, cover and cook over low heat for 5–10 minutes until softened but not coloured. Remove the lid and add the beans and stock. Simmer for 5 minutes. To finish, stir in the mustard, cream and spinach, and season with salt and pepper.

To serve, arrange the mushrooms on a plate and serve with spoonfuls of the creamy beans.

SERVES 2–4

Puréed bean recipes are rich in flavour, taste and nutrients – a good way to serve this unusual and super healthy grain. You can use almost any cooked bean you like here – choose from cannellini, kidney, haricot/navy or butter/lima beans.

bean, cheese & tomato
QUICHES

Preheat the oven to 200°C (400°F) Gas 6.

Put the buckwheat and 300 ml/1½ cups cold water in a large saucepan or pot set over a medium–high heat. Bring to the boil, then reduce the heat and simmer, uncovered, for 7 minutes. Remove from the heat, cover and let stand until all the water has been absorbed.

Meanwhile, put the beans in a food processor with the onion and cream and blend until smooth. Transfer to a mixing bowl and stir in the garlic, sun-dried tomato paste, thyme, tomatoes, cheese and paprika. Season well, then mix to blend. Taste and adjust the seasoning, then stir in the eggs. Set aside until needed.

As soon as the buckwheat is cool enough to handle, press it into the pans, going up the sides, to form a crust. Transfer to a baking sheet and pour in the bean mixture. Bake in the preheated oven for 25–35 minutes, until firm but still wobbly in the middle. Sprinkle with chopped parsley and serve warm with a salad.

150 g/1 cup unroasted buckwheat groats

2 x 410-g/14-oz. cans beans

1 onion, coarsely chopped

165 ml/¾ cup double/heavy cream

1 garlic clove, crushed

2 tablespoons sun-dried tomato paste

1 teaspoon dried thyme

3 tomatoes, coarsely chopped

70 g/1 cup grated vegetarian cheddar

¼ teaspoon paprika

2 eggs, beaten

chopped fresh flat-leaf parsley, to serve (optional)

salt and black pepper

6-8 individual tartlet pans

MAKES 6-8 MINI QUICHES

This wholesome and satisfying pie is the perfect week-night meal and is ideal served with green vegetables or a salad.

ONION PIE

5–6 large onions (a mix of red and white)

2–3 tablespoons olive oil

leaves from a few sprigs of fresh thyme

125 g/1 cup plain/all-purpose flour

125 g/1 cup wholemeal/whole-wheat flour

1 generous teaspoon baking powder

¼ teaspoon salt

75 g/5 tablespoons unsalted butter at room temperature, cut into pieces

150 ml/scant ⅓ cup milk

an enamel-coated ovenproof frying pan/skillet or a non-stick cake pan

Preheat the oven to 200°C (400°F) Gas 6.

Heat the oil in the frying pan/skillet. (If using an ovenproof skillet, you can cook the onions and bake the pie in the same pan. Alternatively, cook the onions in a non-stick frying pan/skillet, then transfer to a cake pan.) When hot, add the onions and thyme and cook over medium heat for 5–8 minutes, stirring occasionally, until soft and lightly browned. Season well. Set aside while you prepare the scone dough.

Put both flours, baking powder and salt in a mixing bowl. Add the butter and rub in with your fingertips to obtain coarse crumbs. Add the milk and stir to obtain a soft dough. Transfer to a lightly floured surface and roll out to a round just larger than the diameter of the pan.

Transfer the dough to the pan, tucking it in around the edges to enclose the onions. Make a few slits in the dough with a sharp knife to allow steam to escape during baking.

Bake in the preheated oven for 20–25 minutes, until the dough is firm and cooked. Let cool for a few minutes, then turn the pie over and cut into slices to serve.

MAKES 6–8 SERVINGS

This is a very simple dish, very impressive and hugely delightful. Time spent peeling and slicing the vegetables is time well spent. Serve with a cheese platter, crusty bread and a green salad.

root vegetable
GRATIN

Preheat the oven to 200°C (400°F) Gas 6.

Put all the vegetable slices in a large bowl and toss gently to combine. Set aside.

Combine the cream, crème fraîche and milk in a small saucepan and heat just to melt the crème fraîche. Stir well, season with salt and pepper.

Arrange half of the vegetables slices in the prepared baking dish. Sprinkle with a little salt and one-third of the cheese. Pour over one-third of the cream mixture. Top with the rest of the vegetable slices, the remaining cheese and a sprinkle of salt. Pour over the remaining cream mixture and bake in the preheated oven for 1–1½ hours, until browned on top.

Serve immediately.

3 small turnips, peeled, halved and very thinly sliced

½ a celeriac, peeled, halved and very thinly sliced

½ a swede, peeled, halved and very thinly sliced

650 g/1 lb. 13 oz. waxy potatoes, peeled, halved and very thinly sliced

225 ml/1 scant cup double/heavy cream

100 g/⅓ cup crème fraîche

250 ml/1 cup milk

125 g/1 cup vegetarian Cheddar, grated

salt and black pepper

a 30 x 20-cm/
12 x 8-inch baking
dish, very well
buttered

SERVES 4–6

GET THE PARTY STARTED!

It may seem strange to add sugar to savoury popcorn, but it really brings out the flavour of the chilli powder and softens the heat slightly.

CHILLI POPCORN

Heat the oil with a few popcorn kernels in a large lidded saucepan or pot set over a medium heat. When you hear the kernels pop, carefully tip in the rest of the kernels and return the lid. Let cook then shake the pan over the heat until the popping stops. Take care when lifting the lid as any unpopped kernels may still pop from the heat of the pan.

Tip the popcorn into a bowl, removing any unpopped kernels as you go.

Shake the salt, chilli powder and sugar in a food bag until you have a mixed fine dust. Sprinkle the chilli mix over the popcorn and squeeze over a little lime juice to bring out the flavour.

Stir well so that the popcorn is evenly coated and serve warm or cold.

1–2 tablespoons vegetable oil

90 g/⅓ cup popcorn kernels

1 teaspoon salt

1 tablespoon chilli powder

2 teaspoons caster/superfine sugar

freshly squeezed juice of 1 lime

MAKES 1 LARGE BOWL

These nifty bite-size morsels are quick to prepare, and delicious dipped in yogurt but no lives will be lost if ketchup is what makes them go down. These reheat well so it's worth making a large batch in advance.

CHICKPEA BITES

Preheat the oven to 200°C (400°F) Gas 6.

Put the onion, carrot, celery and garlic in a food processor and pulse until finely chopped.

Heat the oil in a small non-stick frying pan/skillet set over a medium heat. Add the vegetable mixture, season with salt and pepper and cook for 3–5 minutes, stirring often until soft. Do not allow the mixture to brown or the garlic will taste bitter. Let cool slightly.

Put the chickpeas, mayonnaise, oatbran, flour and orange juice in the food processor and blend, leaving some small chunks of chickpea. The mixture should not be completely smooth. Transfer to a large bowl.

Add the vegetable mixture and stir well. Taste and adjust the seasoning.

Form the mixture into walnut-size balls and arrange on the prepared baking sheet. Bake in the preheated oven for 30–40 minutes, until brown and just golden on top.

Serve, hot, warm or at room temperature with plain yogurt and a sprinkling of fresh herbs.

1 small onion, coarsely chopped

1 carrot, coarsely chopped

1 celery stick, coarsely chopped

1 garlic clove, peeled

2–3 tablespoons olive oil

1 x 410-g/14-oz. can chickpeas, drained and rinsed

2 tablespoons mayonnaise

2 tablespoons oatbran

1 tablespoon wholemeal/ whole-wheat flour

freshly squeezed juice of ½ an orange

salt and black pepper

To serve

plain yogurt

freshly chopped herbs

a non-stick baking sheet, lightly greased

MAKES 12–15 BITES

This velvety smooth sweet potato hoummus dip makes an interesting change from the more familiar chickpea version.

sweet potato
HOUMMUS

1 sweet potato, unpeeled

3 garlic cloves, unpeeled

½ x 400-g/14-oz. can chickpeas

1 fresh red chilli/chile, finely chopped

a handful of fresh coriander/cilantro leaves, chopped

2 tablespoons olive oil

grated zest and freshly squeezed juice of ½ a lime

salt and black pepper

breadsticks, to serve

Preheat the oven to 180°C (350°F) Gas 4.

Roast the sweet potato in a roasting pan for 30–40 minutes until very soft. Add the garlic cloves to the pan about 20 minutes before the end of the cooking time.

Remove from the oven and, when cool enough to handle, remove and discard the skins from the sweet potato and garlic cloves. Put the chickpeas, chilli/chile, coriander/cilantro, olive oil and lime zest in a food processor and blitz until they reach the desired consistency. Season with salt, pepper and lime juice to taste.

Spoon the sweet potato hoummus into a serving bowl and serve with breadsticks for dipping.

SERVES 4-6

Halloumi lends itself to marinating with Mediterranean herbs. It is important to serve these wraps hot while the cheese is soft as it becomes rubbery once cold.

halloumi & pepper
WRAPS

Preheat the grill/broiler to medium.

Mix the olive oil, lemon zest and juice, balsamic vinegar, thyme and black pepper together in a shallow dish. Add the slices of halloumi and set aside to marinate while preparing the peppers.

Put the peppers on the grill rack, skin-side up, and cook until they begin to soften and char. Do not over-cook as they will be cooked again after wrapping. Place in a large bowl, cover and leave for 15 minutes.

Peel the skins off the peppers and remove the stalks and cores. Cut in half lengthways. Put a slice of the marinated halloumi in the centre of each pepper strip, allowing the cheese to protrude slightly over the edges of the pepper. Wrap the pepper over the cheese and secure with a cocktail stick. Put on a shallow baking sheet and brush with the remaining marinade.

Cook under a preheated medium–high grill/broiler for 4–5 minutes on each side, or until the cheese softens and starts to brown and the peppers start to char.

Serve, drizzled with a little salsa verde.

2 tablespoons olive oil

grated zest and freshly squeezed juice of 1 lemon

1 teaspoon balsamic vinegar

2 teaspoons fresh thyme, chopped

225 g/8 oz. halloumi cheese, cut into 12 slices

1 large yellow (bell) pepper, halved lengthways

2 large red (bell) peppers, halved lengthways

black pepper

salsa verde, to serve

MAKES 12
SERVES 4

These fritters are perfect for enjoying with drinks.
You can add feta, herbs and spices for extra flavour.

COURGETTE FRITTERS
with minted yogurt

250 g/3 cups grated courgette/zucchini

4 spring onions/scallions, finely sliced

grated zest and freshly squeezed juice of 1 lemon

1 teaspoon vegetable oil, plus extra for deep-frying

3 tablespoons chickpea flour

1 teaspoon baking powder

salt, to season

minted yogurt, to serve

Sprinkle the courgette/zucchini with salt and put it in a strainer set over a bowl for 10 minutes to draw out any moisture. Rinse the courgette/zucchini well with water to remove the salt, then squeeze out any excess liquid using a clean kitchen towel. Put the drained grated courgette/zucchini in a bowl, add the spring onions/scallions, lemon zest and juice and teaspoon of vegetable oil, and stir till thoroughly mixed. Combine the chickpea flour and baking powder, sprinkle them over the vegetables, then stir until well combined.

These fritters are best made in a deep-fat fryer. If you don't have a deep-fat fryer, put about 2 cm/¾ inch of oil in the bottom of a deep, heavy-bottomed saucepan or pot. Heat the oil until it is 180°C (350°F) – hot but not smoking. The oil is at the correct temperature when a small piece of bread dropped into it takes 40 seconds to turn golden.

Form golf-ball size balls of mixture and drop into the hot oil and cook until golden. Remove the fritters with a slotted spoon and drain on paper towels.

Sprinkle the fritters with salt while they are still hot. They are best eaten immediately but will keep for a short time in a warm oven. Serve with minted yogurt for dipping.

MAKES 4
SERVINGS

LET'S BAKE A CAKE

Blended beans give a wonderful texture to these brownies and it's a great way to introduce plant protein as part of a vegetarian diet. Cashews can be replaced by whatever nuts you have to hand.

bean & cashew
BROWNIES

Preheat the oven to 180°C (350°F) Gas 4.

Melt the chocolate in a heatproof bowl set over a saucepan or pot of simmering water. Do not let the base of the bowl touch the water.

Put the melted chocolate, beans, oil, syrup, lemon juice and zest in a food processor and blend until smooth.

If using whole cashews, finely grind them in a food processor. Mix the flours, ground cashews, baking powder, salt and cinnamon in a mixing bowl. Add the bean mixture and fold using a spatula until you get a smooth, thick consistency (it needs to be much thicker than usual cake mixtures).

Spoon the brownie mixture into the prepared baking pan and spread level with a spatula; if it sticks too much, wet it with warm water and try again.

Bake in the preheated oven for 15–20 minutes. Do not overbake – they are supposed to be a little gooey! Allow to cool completely in the baking pan.

Cut into squares to serve with a little apricot jam/jelly which contrasts beautifully with the rich, heavy chocolate taste of these brownies.

200 g/1½ cups finely chopped dark/bittersweet chocolate (70% cocoa)

300 g/2 cups canned unsalted haricot/navy beans, drained

65 g/⅓ cup sunflower oil

130 g/½ cup maple syrup

freshly squeezed juice and grated zest of 1 lemon

80 g/½ cup whole or 80 g/ 1 cup finely ground cashews

85 g/⅔ cup plain/all-purpose flour

40 g/⅓ cup plain wholemeal/ whole-wheat flour

1 tablespoon baking powder

¼ teaspoon salt

¼ teaspoon ground cinnamon

2 tablespoons apricot jam/jelly, to serve

23 x 30-cm/9 x 12-in. baking pan, oiled

MAKES
ABOUT 20

SERVES 6-8

This is home-cooked comfort at its best. Serve this crumble on a stormy summer evening when there is a bit of rain and wind and everybody feels very shivery and miserable even though it's summertime!

PEACH CRUMBLE

Preheat the oven to 150°C (300°F) Gas 2.

For the crumble, put the nuts in a baking pan and roast them in the preheated oven for 8–10 minutes. Rub off any skins that have loosened from the nuts, then roughly chop the nuts by hand or in a food processor. Big pieces will burn while the crumble is baking, so make them quite small.

Put the flour, oats, zest, cinnamon, vanilla and salt in a bowl and stir. Add the syrup and mix well, then work the margarine in with your hands, rubbing it quickly between your fingers. When the mixture looks crumbly, add the chopped nuts.

Preheat the oven to 180°C (350°F) Gas 4.

Toss the peaches with the apple juice concentrate, flour and salt. Spread them in the ovenproof dish and cover evenly with the crumble.

Bake in the preheated oven for about 35 minutes or until the crumble topping is golden brown and the juice is bubbling up around the edges.

The crumble is best served warm, but if you happen to have leftovers and serve it as a dessert the next day, I'm sure no one will complain!

1.8 kg/about 8 firm but ripe peaches or nectarines, peeled, stoned/pitted and cut into wedges

2–3 tablespoons apple juice concentrate

1 tablespoon plain/all-purpose flour

a pinch of salt

Crumble topping

80 g/½ cup hazelnuts or other nuts

65 g/½ cup plain/all-purpose flour

50 g/½ cup rolled oats

grated zest of 1 orange or lemon

¼ teaspoon ground cinnamon

⅛ teaspoon pure vanilla extract

a pinch of salt

85 g/⅓ cup maple syrup

50 g/⅓ cup margarine, at room temperature

a 2-litre/8-cup ovenproof baking dish

With a trio of chocolate these tiny morsels are a choco-a-holic's dream. You only need to serve small squares as the slice is very rich.

Rocky Road
POPCORN SLICE

1 tablespoon vegetable oil

30 g/2 tablespoons popcorn kernels

30 g/1 oz. shredded/dessicated coconut

100 g/3½ oz. milk/semisweet chocolate, chopped

100 g/3½ oz. dark/bittersweet chocolate, chopped

65 g/4½ tablespoons butter

100 g/2 cups mini marshmallows

150 g/1 cup glacé/candied cherries

Topping

75 g/2½ oz. white chocolate

sugar sprinkles (optional)

18 x 28-cm/7 x 11-inch deep rectangular cake pan, greased and lined with baking parchment

MAKES 24

Heat the oil with a few popcorn kernels in a large lidded saucepan or pot. When you hear the kernels pop, carefully tip in the rest of the kernels. Cover and wait to hear the popping again. Shake the pan over the heat until the popping stops. Take care when lifting the lid as any unpopped kernels may still pop from the heat of the pan. Tip the popcorn into a bowl, removing any unpopped kernels as you go.

In a heavy-based frying pan/skillet, dry roast the shredded/dessicated coconut, stirring all the time, until it starts to colour and give off a nutty aroma. Tip onto a plate and set aside to cool.

Melt the chocolate and butter in a large heatproof bowl set over a saucepan or pot of barely simmering water, making sure that the base of the bowl does not touch the water. Stir the mixture to melt any lumps then remove the bowl from the pan, taking care as it will be hot, and leave to cool for about 10 minutes.

Mix all of the ingredients except the white chocolate and sugar sprinkles together. Spoon the mixture into the prepared pan and press out flat with the back of a spoon.

Melt the white chocolate in a heatproof bowl set over a pan of barely simmering water, and drizzle over the top of the slice. Decorate with sugar sprinkles, if using. Chill in the fridge for 2 hours until set, then cut into 24 small squares and serve.

This blueberry cheesecake is so good you'll want to put your face into it. If you can resist it, serve this to your friends and show off with how good it is.

blueberry
CHEESECAKE

Begin by making the blueberry topping. Simmer the blueberries with the lemon juice and sugar in a saucepan or pot set over a medium heat for about 5 minutes until the fruit has burst and you have a thick sauce. Set aside to cool.

To make the crumb base, crush the biscuits/graham crackers to fine crumbs in a food processor or place in a clean plastic bag and bash with a rolling pin. Transfer the crumbs to a mixing bowl and stir in the melted butter. Press the buttery crumbs into the base of the prepared cake pan firmly using the back of a spoon.

To make the filling, whisk together the mascarpone and crème fraîche in a large mixing bowl until smooth. Sift in the icing/confectioners' sugar, add the lemon zest, then whisk again. Taste the mixture and add a little more icing/confectioners' sugar if you wish it to be sweeter.

Spoon the filling mixture over the crumb base and level with a knife or spatula, then spoon the blueberry topping over the top.

Chill the cheesecake in the refrigerator for at least 3 hours or until set, then cut into slices to serve.

Topping

350 g/2½–3 cups blueberries

freshly squeezed juice of 2 lemons

100 g/½ cup caster/granulated sugar

Crumb base

200 g/7 oz. digestive biscuits/graham crackers

100 g/7 tablespoons butter, melted

Filling

500 g/generous 2 cups mascarpone cheese

500 ml/2 cups crème fraîche

3 generous tablespoons icing/confectioners' sugar, or to taste

grated zest of 2 lemons

a 20-cm/8-inch square loose-based cake pan, greased and lined

SERVES 10

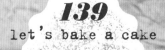

Tangy lemon slices, drenched in a lemon caramel, nestled on top of a delicate lemon sponge, make this cake a must for all citrus lovers.

caramelized
LEMON CAKE

170 g/1½ sticks butter, softened

170 g/¾ cup plus
2 tablespoons caster/
granulated sugar

3 large eggs

115 g self-raising/rising flour

1 teaspoon baking powder

85 g/¾ cup ground almonds

3 tablespoons sour/soured cream

custard sauce or whipped cream, to serve

Caramelized lemons

200 g/1 cup caster/
granulated sugar

freshly squeezed juice of
1 lemon

4 lemons, peeled and sliced, grated zest of 3 reserved

a 25-cm/10-in cast iron tarte tatin pan or a similar heavy, flameproof pan, greased

Preheat the oven to 180°C (350°F) Gas 4.

To make the caramelized lemons, put the sugar and lemon juice in a saucepan or pot set over a medium heat and warm until the sugar melts and turns golden brown. Do not stir whilst cooking but gently shake the pan from time to time to prevent the sugar from burning. Watch closely once the sugar has melted as it will caramelize quickly. Pour into the bottom of the pan. Arrange the lemon slices in the caramel in the pan in a circular pattern – taking care as the caramel will be hot. Set aside.

Put the butter and sugar in a mixing bowl and whisk together until light and creamy. Beat in the eggs and whisk again until the batter is light and airy. Sift in the flour and baking powder and add the ground almonds, sour cream and reserved lemon zest. Fold together until everything is incorporated. Spoon the batter into the pan with the lemon slices.

Bake in the preheated oven for 30–40 minutes, until the cake springs back to the touch and a knife inserted in the middle of the cake comes out clean. Remove from the oven and let cool for a few minutes then put a serving plate on top of the pan and, holding the pan with a kitchen towel turn out the cake onto the plate. Serve warm or cold with custard sauce or whipped cream.

SERVES 8–10

INDEX

RECIPE CREDITS

Ghillie Basan
Carrot, shallot & prune tagine

Jordan Bourke
Puy lentils with aubergine & sun-dried tomatoes
Beetroot burgers
Sweet potato & tomato frittata

Chloe Coker & Jane Montgomery
Vegetarian know-how 13
Caponata
Corncakes with spicy avocado salsa
Courgette fritters
Crunchy oat granola
Hot & sour salad with marinated tofu
Italian-style tear & share bread
Mini bruschettas
Roasted aubergine, sweet potato & spinach curry
Roasted vegetable salad with grilled halloumi
Samosas with lemon & garlic yogurt dip
Stuffed mushrooms with creamy white beans
Sweet potato hoummus
Vegetable & lentil moussaka
Dumplings with dipping sauce
Winter vegetable stew with herbed dumplings

Ross Dobson
Homemade falafel
Greek salad with butter beans
Napolitana lentil stew
Orange veg & spring onion pilau
Simple tomato & basil risotto
Smoky bean hotpot

Felipe Fuentes Cruz & Ben Fordham
Tofu tacos

Tonia George
Homemade baked beans
Bloody Mary
Crumpets
Apple & blackberry porridge

Nicola Graimes
Mexican taco salad

Amanda Grant
Avocado & red pepper sandwich
Egg sandwiches
Homemade pesto
Root vegetable gratin

Dunja Gulin
Bean & cashew brownies
Peach crumble

Hannah Miles
Blueberry cheesecake
Caramelized lemon cake
Chilli popcorn
Rocky road popcorn slice

Louise Pickford
Melon, cucumber & ginger frappé

Annie Rigg
Mushroom & mozzarella arancini

Jennie Shapter
Halloumi & pepper wraps

Laura Washburn
Aromatic Thai curry
Avocado & chickpea wrap
Aubergine parmigiana
Baked rigatoni with mozzarella
Bean, cheese & tomato quiches
Chickpea bites
Cinnamon French toast
Enchiladas
Fruit & nut bars
Greek summer vegetable stew
Multigrain pancakes
Mushrooms on toast
Nutty meatballs
Onion pie
Ratatouille
Root Vegetable Gratin
Squash salad with spiced lentils
Super-nutritious sandwiches
Vegetable & barley soup
Veggie lasagne
Veggie sausage casserole

PHOTOGRAPHY CREDITS

Steve Baxter
Page 53

Martin Brigdale
Page 62, 77, 94, 97, 98, 101, 104, 120

Peter Cassidy
Jkt spine, pages 1, 6, 8-11, 13, 15, 43, 44, 47, 58, 82

Tara Fisher
Pages 39, 40, 54, 55 insert, 122, 137

Jonathan Gregson
Pages 16, 23, 28, 32

Richard Jung
Pages 89, 90, 93

William Lingwood
Page 128

James Merrell
Page 31

Steve Painter
Pages 61, 138

William Reavell
Jkt front, pages 2, 12, 24, 49, 50, 57, 74, 84, 86, 102, 107, 108, 111, 112, 115, 127, 131, 141, 144

Kate Whitaker
Jkt back, pages 5, 7, 14, 19, 20, 27, 34, 36, 65, 66, 68-70, 73, 78, 81, 103, 116, 119, 124

Clare Winfield
Pages 88, 132, 134

MILLS & BOON®
Pure reading pleasure™

NOVEMBER 2008 LARGE PRINT TITLES

ROMANCE

Bought for Revenge, Bedded for Pleasure *Emma Darcy*	978 0 263 20090 4
Forbidden: The Billionaire's Virgin Princess *Lucy Monroe*	978 0 263 20091 1
The Greek Tycoon's Convenient Wife *Sharon Kendrick*	978 0 263 20092 8
The Marciano Love-Child *Melanie Milburne*	978 0 263 20093 5
Parents in Training *Barbara McMahon*	978 0 263 20094 2
Newlyweds of Convenience *Jessica Hart*	978 0 263 20095 9
The Desert Prince's Proposal *Nicola Marsh*	978 0 263 20096 6
Adopted: Outback Baby *Barbara Hannay*	978 0 263 20097 3

HISTORICAL

The Virtuous Courtesan *Mary Brendan*	978 0 263 20172 7
The Homeless Heiress *Anne Herries*	978 0 263 20173 4
Rebel Lady, Convenient Wife *June Francis*	978 0 263 20174 1

MEDICAL™

Nurse Bride, Bayside Wedding *Gill Sanderson*	978 0 263 19986 4
Billionaire Doctor, Ordinary Nurse *Carol Marinelli*	978 0 263 19987 1
The Sheikh Surgeon's Baby *Meredith Webber*	978 0 263 19988 8
The Outback Doctor's Surprise Bride *Amy Andrews*	978 0 263 19989 5
A Wedding at Limestone Coast *Lucy Clark*	978 0 263 19990 1
The Doctor's Meant-To-Be Marriage *Janice Lynn*	978 0 263 19991 8